Re-Run the Fun

Re-Run the Fun

My Life as Pat Sharp

Pat Sharp

with

Darren Richman and Luke Catterson

CONSTABLE

Some of the names might be recognisable but what follows is a work of fiction. You'll see the timeline of the Pat Sharp career with some familiar names and places along the way but everything else is invented.

CONSTABLE

First published in Great Britain in 2020 by Constable

1 3 5 7 9 10 8 6 4 2

Copyright © Pat Sharp, Darren Richman and Luke Catterson, 2020

The moral right of the authors has been asserted.

A CIP catalogue record for this book
is available from the British Library.

ISBN: 978-1-47213-466-0 (hardback)

Typeset in Bembo by Hewer Text UK Ltd, Edinburgh
Printed and bound in Great Britain by Clays Ltd, Elcograf, S.p.A.

Papers used by Constable are from well-managed
forests and other responsible sources.

Constable
An imprint of
Little, Brown Book Group
Carmelite House
50 Victoria Embankment
London EC4Y 0DZ

An Hachette UK Company
www.hachette.co.uk

www.littlebrown.co.uk

This book is dedicated to the funnest of houses.

Contents

'*There are three sides to every story – yours, mine and the truth.*'
Robert Evans

'*Well . . . uh . . . a true story? I couldn't swear to every detail but it's certainly true that it is a story.*'
Sheriff Ed Tom Bell (*No Country for Old Men*)

'*The greatest children's TV presenter ever to have lived.*'
Neil Buchanan (admittedly talking about himself)

'*Oh, the mullet guy?*'
Various (admittedly talking about Pat Sharp)

Prologue

It can't be true. As I stand on the set one last time and contemplate the end of an era, it occurs to me that it simply cannot be true.

It's late 1999 and we're just days away from a legendary Millennium Eve party chez Sharp, but my mind couldn't be further from the prospect of sitting around my computer with friends and family waiting for it to crash.

Neil Buchanan was present and kept banging on about Internet dating and how he'd landed a stunner. It would transpire he was the first victim of 'catfishing', but refused to be interviewed for the television show.

It's hard to believe I've been doing this job for ten years and even harder to believe it's all about to come to an end. 'Every new beginning comes from some other beginning's end . . .' went the Semisonic song I was rarely allowed to play on London's Heart a year earlier. How I'd fought the men upstairs on that one. How I'd lost. Still, I'd won with 'Sweet Like Chocolate' and I still get Christmas cards from Shanks and Bigfoot. Was this closing time for Sharpy or a new beginning? In time, the answer to that question would become patently obvious.

The whole thing feels like a dream. We've done this hundreds of times before and yet today things feel very different and there is a definite sadness behind Melanie's eyes – or maybe it was Martina's – I never really bothered learning which twin was which. At the end of round one, I wipe something from my eye but, on this solitary occasion, it's not a stray bit of gunge. 'Keep it together, Pat – the show must go on,' the twins tell me, with the waving of their pom-poms. 'Keep it together, Pat – the show must go on,' the producer tells me with the earpiece in my ear.

Everything is a blur of red and yellow. The names of the obstacles are suddenly imbued with profound meaning after years of seeming little more than gibberish: The Snake in the Box, Fireman's Pole, Flying Fox, Ball Run, Climbing Net, A-Frame, Giant Steps, Danger Net, Crawl Tube, WildSlide. The list is endless. Although I'm going to end it there.

Gunge is no longer merely a gooey slime with thick, viscous consistency – it is the very stuff of life itself. We are all of us a disgusting runny substance but some of us are looking at the stars. Most of us live in a house but it takes that something special to make it a Fun one.

We've done 139 episodes. That's fewer than *EastEnders* but more than *Knightmare*; fewer than *The Really Wild Show* but more than the 1994 FA Cup Final. You might think they all blur into one but they don't. Each one is a vivid and distinct memory. Like a snowflake, the untrained eye considers them the same but the beauty is in the nuance.

It is during the final round when I come closest to losing it. This has been my life for a decade, a non-stop rollercoaster of shrieking children and ageing twins. And now it's coming to an end. The final prepubescent competitors ('prepubescitors' was the popular industry term Chris Tarrant once proudly claimed to have coined) enter the Fun House and seek their fortune. Not literally, obviously – the only prizes in there were non-monetary because of an obscure European law stating that children cannot win money on game shows.

The red team exit with an incredible array of riches, ranging from a state-of-the-art Sony Discman to a state-of-the-art Sony Walkman. They didn't get the stationery kit but then you can't always get what you want. But now it's time for an action replay, one last glimpse of the Red Boy's incredible lunge across the ball pool. 'Let's . . .' I begin, before taking a moment to compose myself and utter the words I'd said so many times before. The words which I knew then would make the perfect title for my autobiography: '. . . re-run the fun!'

Chapter 1

Tom Jones – 'Sugar Sugar'

Probably the only person who could be called a 'pants magnet' and still be cool, how do you not pick Tom Jones? I know it's the obvious choice but it's hard to overlook the song he is almost synonymous with – his cover of 'Sugar Sugar'.

I was born Patrick Sharpin in October 1961. A beginning is something you only get to do once because, after that, it isn't a beginning any more, but more of a middle, on the way to becoming an end. One of Mum's little proverbs, that. She would never use one word if a hundred would do and that ability to fill the silence was something I inherited and stood me in good stead when interviewing monosyllabic pre-teens many years later.

My parents were incredibly proud when I was born. Our neighbours had offered a lift to the hospital but my father steadfastly refused saying, 'We can take care of everything, thank you very much.' He maintained that the Robinsons were the type of people who would never let you forget they'd done you a favour, although I never saw any evidence of that.

The upshot of all this was that I was born at home; in the games room, to be exact, but 'not too close to the pool table . . . I don't know if embryonic fluid will come out of the baize'.

5

Did the fact that I was born in the 'fun' room of the house have any bearing on my future career? It seems a little ridiculous to say so and yet I feel that it would be remiss not to bring it up.

My mother tells me I made quite the entrance. More often than not, as I watched a contestant emerge from the giant spinning foam towers that marked the threshold of the Fun House, panting and reaching out for the studio floor, I would wonder how much my birth looked like that. It's impossible to say for sure but you have to assume rather a lot.

It was a quick labour, which I like to think of as the equivalent of jumping into shot in a sort of 'Ta-da!' fashion (something I would later make entirely my own). Our makeshift midwife was my mum's friend and she maintains that I really 'held the room'. Had I had the power of speech I know for a fact I would have given a breezy greeting before engendering a rousing reception for the first guest: 'Ladies and gentleman, please give it up for . . .the placenta!'

I actually don't know what happened to that placenta. I still think about it sometimes.

I was the eldest child of one and enjoyed a very pleasant if unremarkable early life. We lived in Marylebone, London. The station isn't as important to the infrastructure of London as the board game Monopoly would have you believe, but it's still a thoroughly nice place.

My mother was a cleaner and one of my earliest memories was being taken with her to one of her jobs. She would sit me in a baby seat where I would be quite happy entertaining myself. Sometimes, the clients would be in or would come home while we were still there. I'd attract a lot of attention, especially with my thick, luxurious locks that were already in abundance. By the time I started nursery, it was found that I was in the top one percentile for hair. A lot of fuss was made about how I was a 'delight', 'no trouble at all' and 'a refreshing personality that is likely to resonate with a range of demographics through multiple mediums'. Though they were good to me, they were often not so kind to my mother and I remember them shouting and everything becoming very heated. It was only years later that I was able to understand fully the injustice of those exchanges, when I was old enough to see what a shocking job my mother did as a cleaner. Most of her scrubbing was nothing short of a disgrace.

Those memories all merge together but there's one afternoon that really sticks out. My mother was sitting on the sofa after a tiring ten minutes flapping a duster in the vague direction of some cabinets when she said some words that flew into my six-year-old core like an old car door to a junkyard magnet. 'There's so much bloody mess here . . . I hope they had fun making all that mess because it's a bugger to sort it all out.' My six-year-old brain took that sentence, cropped it, cleaned it up and identified the wonderful idea at its heart. What my mother had been trying to say, in her typically cack-handed way, was that she hoped they'd had fun making all that mess. I didn't quite know what it meant but I knew that it was important. It was the start of something. Something big.

In the car on the way home, I realised that the big something was a game. Making mess was fun but tidying away wasn't. What if I could devise a way that people could play and make as much mess as they wanted without worrying about tidying up? I had the title almost immediately and, as I'm sure you know, dear reader, the show would end up being made in the late '80s.

It wasn't straightforward and the show was in development hell for quite a few years. I was beginning to think that the show I knew I would become known for in years to come was simply going to disappear into obscurity, but they were able to get Sam Fox involved when she was really struggling for work. The final product was nothing at all like I'd originally envisaged and they pretty much only used the title but, sadly, that is all too often the way that things go in the entertainment business. Still, I probably never would have come up with *Fun House* if we'd gone ahead with *Filthy, Dirty – Why Don't You Come and Make a Mess?*

The other thing that I remember about those days watching my mother do a sub-standard job of cleaning people's houses was listening to the radio. The first thing my mother would do was to find the wireless and stick it on full blast. In fact, most of the cleaning she did was inadvertently sweeping by dancing around in her socks. There are so many things that make radio brilliant – the way that it comforts, the way that it stirs the imagination, opens new worlds that can only open because of the restrictions of it, notably being audio. One of those benefits is the way that it can introduce you to new things. It's the outside world entering yours – pouring people, art, ideas into your world and you can take as much or as little as you like.

It was through the radio that I first encountered The Beatles. 'Penny Lane' was the latest single and it hit my ears like a custard pie hitting a clown's face. The way the DJ announced it and seamlessly segued into a letter from a reader. It was like nothing I'd ever heard – casual, smooth, engaging, playful, uplifting, respectful. His voice was like velvet dripping in butter running down a water slide but with the flow restricted just enough to create the occasional moment of deeply satisfying roughness. Even today when I hear 'Penny Lane', part of me hopes that it will end with one of the best aural experiences of my life but, alas, it can never be replicated. I also think the song is all right but I largely think of it as an obstacle standing between me and the voice of an angel. An angel by the name of Tony Blackburn.

I liked school. Straight away I took to it like a duck to water and I think it was probably because I was suddenly presented with an audience. It's a bit of a cliché to say that I was the class presenter but that's very much how it was. I was always standing up and hyping whoever came into the room and, if ever something needed to be introduced, then everybody knew to expect my smooth voice and waving hands. It's another cliché to say that I used presenting to win over the bullies but that's again very much how it was. They'd come over to ask for my lunch money and I'd ask them engaging questions designed to give them a platform to tell an anecdote and then I'd whip up any nearby onlookers into a frenzy of applause and cheering. The key was always energy. I found early on that if you ask people questions that are fairly inane but require slightly more than a 'yes' or 'no' response, then they'll think you're a bit strange – but if you do it with enough energy, then people go with it. I began experimenting with generic but positive nick-names like 'big man' at this stage and, it's safe to say, I haven't looked back.

I knew everybody at school. I knew all of their names, all of their favourite subjects, all of their favourite popstars. Every break time, I would flit from person to person having high-octane conversations for about twenty seconds before diving off to see a new person and showing them how excited I was that they were around before hurling myself at somebody else for some rapid-fire chatter.

I liked being in class. Shouting out continuity announcements between different parts of the lesson was a highlight for me and I think everybody liked how I kept the energy up and things stayed light. 'Wow, question three was hilarious . . . Steve certainly looks like he got in a bit of a mess there. Let's see what that's done to the scores!' There were two boys, Tim and Carl, who I had nominated to be scorers but they didn't ever actually keep score. It didn't matter because there were no prizes on offer and, although their lack of professionalism surprised and disappointed me at first, it made me realise that I was different. I demanded perfection and commitment and I had a sneaking suspicion that it would take me a long way. A very long way.

The playground was my favourite, though. I loved the freedom of running all over the place. Like I said about radio, it's a window to the whole world and you have access to everything. The playground felt like that to me. When you're six, you can't even imagine being seven so an area a third the size of a football pitch feels like the whole world with its sights and sounds and smells, and I just wanted to be in the middle of it all.

The one place I didn't like being was on the bus. We used to have school trips quite frequently and those journeys probably weren't very long but they felt interminable to me. I wasn't used to sitting in one space for so long and, unlike the classroom, it wasn't in the round. People would sit in pairs and tended only to talk to the person next to them. It's strange to think how we change. I think one of the big differences between childhood and adulthood is how much you want to sit next to somebody on a bus. For the whole journey! I couldn't do that – primarily because nobody tended to sit next to me. It was when we were on our way to the Science Museum that it occurred to me that I was a Jack of all friends, master of none.

My favourite thing was when there was a new kid starting school. I was always called upon to meet them and show them around. I'd make them feel immediately at ease by jumping up and down in front of them and rattling off quick-fire questions. Then I'd get to introduce them to people and I always did a magnificent job. No sooner had I introduced them to somebody, and it didn't even seem to matter if they had nothing in common, that was it – they would be off talking to their new buddy and walking swiftly away from me as if that person was their best friend in the world.

On one occasion, I sat next to Jason Nethercott on the bus for reasons that I've forgotten. We had a great first couple of minutes as we chatted and laughed, although I was doing the lion's share of both of those activities. It came as something of a surprise when he snapped and told me that I was being annoying. Me? I was the one doing all of the work. I was asking the questions, I was making the glib and lively responses and bringing all of the energy to our two-person seat and yet he had the temerity to say that he wished he didn't have to sit next to me. It's never a nice feeling when somebody says that to you. It hurts when it's Jason Nethercott on a school bus and it hurts when it's everyone on your table at the Brits.

While the abuse at the Brits was haphazard and impersonal, Jason cut to the quick. He looked me up and down, from my glorious head of hair to my monogrammed trainers and said something that pains me to type even now, all these years later.

'You put the prick in Patrick.'

Ouch. I had already been wondering if my name was slightly too long and needed some tidying up (typical Mum), but now my decision was made for me. From that day forth, I would be known simply as Pat. Pat Sharpin.

It was only a temporary setback. Even then I felt like a wise head, like I was the sort of person who understood people. Jason wasn't angry at me. I was just the closest person when he needed to lash out. In retrospect, we were going to the Science Museum yet again and Jason's favourite subject was trigonometry and we never seemed to get around to visiting the Trigonometry Museum.

I did fairly well at school without being spectacular. My mother would later remark that it was little surprise that I ended up on Radio 1 and *Top of the Pops* seeing as my reports were always so full of Bs and Cs. She would repeat the joke later when looking at one of my payslips. 'I thought for a minute this was one of your old school reports!' I found the joke just amusing enough to overlook the fact that she'd opened my post.

It's strange that it's only looking back now that I realise that I didn't have any close friends. It's sad, I suppose, but it didn't seem that way at the time. Luckily, things are far less tragic these days. It's only occurred to me now, as I sit here in this café alternating between writing these pages and pressing F5 on my inbox to see if the University of Roehampton have changed their mind about booking me to be part of their freshers' week, that I realise you sometimes don't appreciate just how upsetting your situation is. Poor little Pat.

I'd still go to sleepovers and birthday parties at bowling alleys but that was part of the inherent agreement that invitations will be extended to everyone in your class. I sometimes think that life would be simpler if we kept that system and just stayed in our primary school classes through life. It would be great to have such a self-contained guest list for your wedding.

I can remember being absolutely stunned by the behaviour I witnessed at one birthday bash. A few of us lads were round at Peter Hancock's house and I couldn't believe it when they started baking brownies. Then, as if overcome by sheer joy, they started giggling uncontrollably after each bite. It's really amazing to me that men who came of age in the 1970s in this country are often considered an unenlightened breed and yet my peers found such joy in the act of baking.

So I never really had a best friend but I did have a worst. I wouldn't say that Kevin Holt was a bully but he really seemed to have less a chip and more an oversized King Edward potato on his shoulder when it came to me. I would always greet him the same way I greeted everybody: big smile, cheery shouting of his name, arm round the shoulder and talking to him from slightly above and behind. He would always shake off my arm, though, and talk to me through gritted teeth.

I suspected that he didn't like me but it was only when he challenged me to a fight that I knew for sure. The challenge was made in the middle of morning break in a public arena meaning it was impossible to turn down. As the exciting 'oohing' from the playground reached a crescendo, I realised that I had no choice but to accept. As an only child, the honour of my family, much like my hair in its heyday, rested on my shoulders. I knew that I had an obligation to fight for my family's name (that I would later change to make slightly snappier).

The fight was arranged for after school that day and went the way of all of those types of fights. There was a lot of hype and excitement and then some jostling and hair pulling. I still wasn't really sure why we were fighting so, before the jostling and hair pulling stage, I simply watched Kevin and waited for some kind of explanation. I didn't really get it – he just kept shouting, 'I hate you!' which was disconcerting because he was looking slightly above my eyeline. The crowd goaded us and I heard bets being taken. The consensus seemed to be that I was slight favourite because of my energy levels and movement but, if Kevin caught me, then it could get ugly pretty quickly.

The 'fight' itself was an equal division of labour – I did the jostling and he did the hair pulling. At one stage, he had me in a kind of headlock and it was like he was rubbing his face into my hair and I was sure that I detected the faint sound of sobbing. 'Sheet, blad . . . some kid's gettin' deaded,' remarked Mr Moorhouse, our Head of English.

Only when we were separated by Mr Moorhouse, did I notice that Kevin's hair was starting to thin. The way it was dishevelled made the recession of the hairline that bit more obvious. Suddenly, it all made sense.

I suppose it was then I realised that my hair would one day come to prominence. Great prominence.

My father held down a number of different jobs. He started out as a single-glazing salesman but felt like he couldn't keep up with the technological advances of the industry. He would later be a tree surgeon and vociferously deny that he was a gardener, even though all he really ever did was cut people's lawns.

The jobs I most associate with him, though, are that of a fireman and, before that, a bailiff. He used to tell me stories about his day and where I should hide my most valuable possessions if I ever got myself into unmanageable debt by buying too many holidays and fridges.

A couple of times, he took me with him so that I could be 'an extra pair of hands' and 'help reduce the chances of extreme violence this time'. One afternoon in particular sticks in my mind. A family hadn't paid any of their bills for three years and they continued to buy things on various credit cards. A team of five of us barged our way into the house. 'Steve – electricals; Tony – jewellery; Colin – first editions of Victorian novels.'

The man of the house made token efforts to stop Steve taking the television but soon realised that it was futile. There were four men who were much bigger than him, and they had the law on their side. He slumped to the floor and put his head in his hands. His wife emerged and was hysterical. She pleaded and begged for forgiveness. 'Please, that armchair was my grandfather's,' she sobbed. Two young children came out and asked what was happening. 'Why is the man taking all of our games?' squeaked a tubby boy who mashed his face into his mother's hip rather than receive an answer.

By the time Colin emerged with a signed copy of George Mcdonald's 1855 dramatic poem 'Within and Without', the house had more or less been gutted and my dad was satisfied that there was enough in the van to cover the family's debts.

As I tiptoed across the strewn books and remaining possessions of minimal value, I thought about how much fun it had been to run around the house and grab interesting items and, as I gave the family whose home had been gutted a cheerful wave (that wasn't returned), I remember thinking, 'There's a children's game show in this.' And so there would be.

I suppose you could say that that initial memory also laid down the foundations for *Fun House*, which was far more successful than *Family Credit Card Disaster* ever was. I didn't make the connection at the time but we essentially replaced tearful families with smiling twins, and urns containing the ashes of loved ones with a combined TV/video player and, from then on, there was no looking back. Until the show was cancelled in 1999, from which point I would look back pretty much constantly.

I feel there's little else I need to tell you about my early childhood, save for this one story. The story of my first school dance.

I went to an all-boys school and it's funny to me now that that seems like such an alien prospect to a lot of people. People ask me, 'What was that like?' and I never really know how to respond. After several years of fielding the query, I think I've finally come up with a succinct and accurate articulation of the all-boy experience – it's like any other school except all the girls are also boys.

The thing that a lot of people say about all-boys schools is that it further mystifies the great unknown quantity that is the fairer sex but, personally, I don't think it makes that much difference. Being in the same room as girls while they're learning how to do algebra doesn't make it any easier to ask them out or express yourself suavely when in their presence. Personally, I've always been OK with women. I realise that I'm very lucky and I certainly appreciate it but they've never filled me with terror, and I've always been able to talk to them without too much trouble. I don't have any stories of tripping up on my way to ask a girl out, or saying something embarrassing in front of the whole class.

Those things happened to my friends. There was a park that was roughly halfway between our school and a girls' school so it would serve a bit like no man's land in the war. It was more like the Cold War than the First World War with a lot of posturing but little in the way of actual conflict. Trevor once 'went over the top' when he shouted to Victoria Lewis who was at the top of the steps in the park. Having got her attention, he attempted to scale them two at a time with a view to arriving at the summit breathless, whereupon he would ask her if she wanted to 'hold hands in the bushes or whatever'. He lost his front teeth on the fourth step and his dignity forever more. He's happily married now and we don't talk about it, but it's clear his soul is still hurting.

Simon was very good at making Susan Turner laugh and, when a large crowd was eavesdropping, expressed the satisfaction he took from this by saying, 'You make me feel funny.' The echoing laughter seemed never to end. He is not happily married and we often talk about how damaging that experience has been to him.

I suppose the key for me was never to overthink things. I didn't worry what the girls would think or what I would say. I treated them like my friends – superficially and with little to no lasting or meaningful interaction. I would ask their favourite subject, I would whoop and holler and get those around me to do the same, and I would move on.

There's only really one thing that I remember about that dance. It was the first time I fell in love and everything changed. It's a bit cringeworthy to put it like that but I don't know how else to. The lyrics to the songs on the London's Heart playlist may sound a bit trite and saccharine at times but, however naff they might be perceived to be, there's no denying that they're true. Apart from 'Insania' by Peter Andre. That's just gibberish.

The moment was as cheesy as you might imagine. I walked into the community hall and everybody seemed to part, giving me the perfect view of her as she stood proudly at the other end of the room. My heart stopped for a second and I wondered what her name was. I would later find out it was the Sony M2 2-channel mixer. She was playing Boney M, and 'Rasputin' had never sounded so magical. At the age of fourteen, I finally knew how I would spend the rest of my life.

Chapter 2

Slade – 'Mama Weer All Crazee Now'

I don't think Slade get enough credit for being the role models they were. They told millions of kids that even if you can't spell and have a weird taste in hats, you can still make it. Would we have Boy George without Dave Hill?

It is a truth universally acknowledged that a single man in possession of a good barnet must be in want of a mobile disco.

The problem – as is so often the case in matters of extreme social importance – was that of money. I didn't have any. My parents, a perfunctory cleaner and a mediocre fireman respectively, didn't have a lot more. My adolescence was far from ideal.

The thing is, I knew I had a gift. In the way that beautiful people have beauty or funny people have funny, I oozed presenter from every orifice – predominantly mouth but not exclusively. There wasn't a social situation I couldn't enliven with my natural ability. That isn't meant to sound arrogant, it's just the truth. There would be times when Mum and Dad would have friends over and call up the stairs, 'Patrick, come and do your Noel Edmonds.' I would race down the stairs, hair bouncing up and down behind me and enter the living room with a flourish.

'It's just coming up to half-past eight, that was the Bay City Rollers with "You Made Me Believe in Magic".'

I could tell from the baffled expressions on the faces of my parents' friends that they were expecting an impression of some kind. I could also tell, from pure intuition, that this would live longer in the memory than any bit of mere mimicry. Tonight, in bed, just before they turned out the light, the husband was bound to turn to his wife and say, 'That kid really had something. I mean, we hadn't heard "You Made me Believe in Magic" by the Bay City Rollers, but I really felt like we had.' And his other half would no doubt agree while envying my hair's natural volume.

I told Noel Edmonds about this in the BBC canteen years later and he really got a kick out of it. He told me he was so amused that he wasn't even going to pursue any potential copyright infringement issues. I framed the story as an example of my parents being a bit annoying, but Noel was quick to point out that he'd gladly swap his for mine. Quick as a flash, I replied, 'No deal!' We both laughed but I regretted the joke when I thought about it afterwards – Noel had looked impossibly sad and I knew his dad had never really recovered from his involvement in the bombing of Dresden and things were a bit fraught between the two.

There was one occasion when I was practising a link in my bedroom, something like 'Here's Geraldine with the weather. Don't suppose you've got any sun for us, have you, Gezza?' when Mum shouted up the greatest eight words in the English language: 'Pat, can you turn that bloody radio off!' If I could fool Mum, one of the biggest fans of the medium there's ever been and also the person who heard my voice the most, the world was my oyster. I cherished what I thought was an incredibly unique and special moment until *Stars in their Eyes* started on telly and I found every contestant had exactly the same story. My tale was better, though, because those people could merely sing – I could *present*. The average drive time will have music from thirty to forty artists, but there will only be one presenter. That's basic maths.

Since my parents couldn't help and I desperately needed money, I decided to write to my heroes and ask for advice. As a teenager, your idols always seem larger than life somehow, but I'm proud to say that both the men I wrote to still hold a special place in my heart – God bless Mr Boney M and Mr Terry W.

I cannot put into words my excitement when Boney replied within a couple of weeks. Emails are all well and good but there's nothing quite like tearing open an envelope and devouring the contents within. Unfortunately, Mum chucked out a box with loads of my old things when I left home so I no longer have the letter, but I can remember the key components. Mr M began with some strange joke about that not being his actual name (classic Boney and his weird sense of humour – only he could have written a song as peculiar as 'Daddy Cool'). Then there were words like 'cease' and 'desist', questions about how I got the address and a couple of phrases I wouldn't want to include in a family-friendly book. There wasn't a lot to go on, but I was pretty good at reading between the lines even then and I realised what I had to do – I needed to get a job and save up for a mobile disco. Cheers Bonester, I owe you one! I heard nothing from Wogan.

The need to raise money was an annoying stumbling block. It's not that I'm averse to hard graft by any means (we used to record an entire series of *Fun House* in a week, don't forget), but I felt it was a distraction from my art. If an athlete goes a day without training, he will complain of withdrawal symptoms. Comedians don't like to take a night off gigging because they think they'll go rusty. So it was with me and my cassette deck. Without it, I wasn't sure who I was.

Like most kids of my generation, I mastered the art of recording the Top 40 on a Sunday night and skilfully editing it. I would listen carefully with my finger poised over the stop button ready to pounce and make sure not to get any music whatsoever. I was honing my craft.

The summers never seemed to end back then. I can remember countless hours spent standing in front of the mirror in my room with a hairbrush in hand. I was brushing my hair, obviously.

I was seventeen and I had the devotion of a sportsman coupled with the heart of an artist. Friends would implore me to come out on Friday nights and hit the town but I just wasn't interested. What could girls possibly offer me that a perfectly formed jingle could not? I cringe when I think of some of my early efforts using phrases like 'Pat FM' and 'BBC Radio Pat' but, no doubt, Roger Federer feels the same way when he ponders his teenage backhand. Greatness is not achieved overnight.

We'll never know if Fed used his sumptuous backhand technique to chuck newspapers at letterboxes but we do know that I had no option – a paper round seemed to be the answer to my prayers. My body might have been cycling through the mean streets of Edgware in the bracing cold but my mind was somewhere else entirely – presenting a breakfast show that was all smooth segues and perfectly timed fade-ins. 'Bliss was it in that dawn to be alive but to be young was very heaven!' I really needed to stop quoting lines of poetry if I was ever going to make it on to Radio 1.

I started to drop subtle hints at home whenever I could. Breakfast would rarely pass without me saying something along the lines of, 'Boy, I really do wish I had the cash to afford a mobile disco . . .' or 'I think the only thing I need in life is a mobile disco or the money to buy it.' You cannot fathom the depths of my despair on Christmas morning 1978 when I received my present – a golden Labrador puppy. Every wag of his tail seemed like a taunt. A dog may well be for life but, to me, it felt closer to death. Discovering life isn't fair was a brutal lesson not dissimilar to learning that Father Christmas wasn't real – common sense and not that big a deal. Still, why couldn't the future just begin already?

I grew older, seasons changed and my hair grew more lustrous. I was getting too old to be rattling around on a push bike delivering papers, so I dipped into my sacred treasure fund to make the step into adulthood and picked up a cheap second-hand motorbike, leaving my Raleigh Chopper behind. It had an immediate impact and I turned many a head. In a few short months, I also left the paper round behind because I needed a fresh challenge and grew tired of the taunts. I'd had enough of the tediousness of picking up my paper bag, taking the papers and delivering them. I needed a new way of earning money that was completely unrecognisable from my previous job. I became a motorcycle dispatch rider. I was way ahead of the curve, riding around in leather years before Wham! made it cool. And years after.

I must confess, dear reader, it was at this point that I started to become disillusioned with the whole thing. I had sent my tapes out to a variety of agents and not heard back, all the while spending three-quarters of the money I earned on hair products. I was at my lowest ebb when a letter came through the door that would change my life for ever. A letter that was never consigned to the box Mum threw out. A letter that I am looking at as I type, behind its glass frame in my study. Here's what Terry wrote back:

Dear Pat,

Thanks so much for your letter. Sorry it's taken me so long to reply, there was a fair bit of fan mail to get through and I knew your correspondence required a little more concentration on my part.

Firstly, to answer your questions – yes, yes, no, maybe, it's my real hair, yes, on occasion and so long as it doesn't contain nuts. Thank you for the tape, you have a real gift and no doubt will put me out of a job one of these days. How that hasn't happened already is a mystery to us all but perhaps one day they'll actually listen to my show and it's people like you that they'll want to find. I hope you don't mind but I've passed your tape on to a few producers here at the BBC because it's clear you deserve a wider audience and, should any of the regular presenters need some time off, I've been assured they'll give you a call. Also, because children in need are close to my heart, I've attached a cheque that should help you put down a deposit on the mobile disco you so desire. Now go out there and do me proud.

Your friend and future colleague,
Michael Terence Wogan

Even reading it back now, for the millionth time, I have tears in my eyes. Lucky old angels, lucky old heaven.

Fast forward a few weeks and I am standing in front of a large crowd of people playing Dexys Midnight Runners and The Nolans. I feel completely empowered and the random sequence of flashing lights makes this feel like a broadcast from my very soul. Unfortunately, it starts to rain and a helpful punter suggests I should go inside the garden centre. An even more helpful punter tells me that garden centres might not be the answer at all and that I should DJ at school discos, weddings, bar mitzvahs . . . And DJ them I shall.

I was a machine in those early days. At my peak, I was gigging three or four times a week and twice a day on weekends. Like David Bowie, I experimented with different voices, different personas, different hairstyles (OK, I admit that last one is a lie – you don't mess with perfection). I felt like I was growing up in public and having the courage to fail is something that's important for anyone in a creative industry. There's not a single mistake I wouldn't relive in a heartbeat because they all helped to make me the broadcaster I am today. Apart from the time I took my Bowie fascination too far and wore Nazi regalia while DJing a bar mitzvah. That was a mistake.

I was making a name for myself in the London area but my aspirations were greater than that. School was tough because I had no interest in my work and spent every waking hour daydreaming about a life on the airwaves (something my Physics teacher insisted was not possible). I would idly write the names of my heroes on the desk in felt-tip pen so that future generations might remember those legendary figures: Diddy David Hamilton, Kid Jensen, Mike Read. These men were titans and the sooner this kid could become the next Kid, the better.

Jason Nethercott, the bully from Chapter 1, still hated me with a passion. Children can be so cruel and he would delight in pronouncing 'disc jockey' as 'knob jockey'. It was absurd. He knew perfectly well I wasn't riding any knobs but he went ahead and said it anyway.

If school was bad then home was . . . also bad. My parents had saved up every penny they had to have me privately educated at Merchant Taylors' School but they barely recognised me as their son once things starting taking off. One night, things came to a head over dinner.

'We barely recognise you as our son since things started taking off,' said Dad. Mum agreed.

'You just seem like such a dandy these days . . . all these affectations just to try and look cool.'

I was so livid I removed my sunglasses and took the pipe out of my mouth. These people would never understand me. Yes, I might have been squeezed out of the vagina of one of them but we were strangers under the same roof. The dog was no better, consistently barging into my room unannounced and barking while I was attempting to record demo drive-time shows.

'I bet Kenny Everett never had to put up with this crap!' I snapped. Snapping is the one thing you have to avoid at all costs as a broadcaster (that and striking someone in a non-playful fashion) but their incessant questioning had pushed me over the edge. If I was losing my cool at this stage of my career, what hope did I have of dealing with screaming children on a sweltering studio floor?

When I think back to that moment now, I feel a combination of pride and shame not dissimilar to doing a really big poo. It is a feeling I would become acquainted with again and again as the years passed and I reflected on my career. I was proud to have got my point across to my parents since their biggest problem was that they lacked ambition. I used to say to Dad that he probably stood in front of the mirror as a kid playing air bass. The shame, however, was very real given I owed these people everything and I couldn't manage to get through one admittedly poorly prepared shepherd's pie without losing my rag.

On a more positive note, it was around that time that everything came together for me in a professional sense. There was one gig that stands out in which everything coalesced perfectly in a glorious cacophony of light, sound and beauty. Sportsmen often talk about being in the zone, that ephemeral moment where they feel touched by God and nothing can harm them. So it was for me in a derelict sports hall in Hatch End as I played 'The Birdie Song' to an audience of seven-year-olds. I might have been as good as that on a handful of occasions since, but I'm not sure I've ever been better. At one point they went ballistic. Some of the mothers put it down to E numbers, but some of us knew that it was the dose of pure Pat. My tunes and banter were like catnip to them. Patnip, if you will (forget Tarrant – that one's all mine).

I had the mobile disco, I had the clothes, I had the hair. I had mastered my craft. Now all I needed was an opportunity. There was only one game I was worse at than Subbuteo and that was the waiting game. But I had no choice. Why wouldn't one of the regular BBC radio presenters just take a holiday already? Then, one majestic spring day, I received a correspondence that would change my life for ever – a letter of such breathtaking power that I used to keep it close to my heart for good luck. News doesn't get any better.

It was from the British Broadcasting Corporation. Bruno Brookes had been rushed to hospital.

Chapter 3

Adam Ant – 'Goody Two Shoes'

I don't drink, I don't smoke and plenty of people have asked me, 'What do you do?' Adam Ant was another great role model, proving that if you are really attractive and charismatic, you can still make it. Such a sexy man. Woof!

Fortunately, there was nothing seriously wrong with Bruno Brookes. The injury had come halfway through the show when he made one of his trademark quips and one of his in-studio team only half-chuckled at it. Bruno's a professional so he was able to make it to the end of the show but it was clear that something wasn't right and, if you listen back, you can hear from his voice that he is clearly in quite a lot of pain. He actually drove himself to Casualty and, when he checked himself in at the desk, they told him his injury was minor enough that there was no point him waiting around and he should just go home to rest.

Apparently, there is no treatment for dented confidence. Personally, I think the staff were a little cruel not to guffaw uncontrollably and firmly believe that Bruno did the right thing by playing it safe and going to get himself checked out.

I know there are people that will think that I'm a sidekick apologist. Even now, I have people come up to me and ask how it is that there is a breed of people (their words not mine. I'm not sure it's a specific 'breed') that can find slightly amusing comments hysterically funny. How do these people manage to do it at half-six in the morning? Why must they make us feel humourless for merely raising a smile when they struggle for breath like life has peaked at the pinnacle of amusement? Like one of those infuriating cheap crossword books, I don't have the answers. What I can say is that the in-studio team provide a vital role. I'm not going to look for sympathy and say that being a DJ or broadcaster is a hardship. It is a wonderful, wonderful job that I have been privileged to do. What I would like to say is that just because something is brilliant, doesn't mean that sometimes it isn't hard.

It's a weird thing being in the studio. You know that you're being transmitted into the homes and lives of hundreds or thousands or even millions of people, but you get no sense of it in that little box of records and wires. These days, it's a little bit different with all the monitors displaying emails and social media but, even so, it's often difficult to comprehend the fact that people are in their cars taking their kids to school, or doing the washing up, or sitting in the garden while you speak directly to them. It was even harder back in the early '80s when you would only have phone calls or letters. You're painfully aware of the scale of our audience and yet you have no way to engage directly with them. A lot of the greats, like Terry, imagine talking to one person, which is why it sounds so personal and special, but it's so hard to know if you're doing well. You doubt yourself. All the time, even the greats. You can't imagine Kenny Everett cringing as Bananarama plays and he wonders if his last link was any good, but I can guarantee he did. So, it may sound a bit over the top and sycophantic but having somebody in the studio with you, validating what you're doing and giving you something to feed off, a shot in the arm, is more important than I can adequately express here. Admittedly, Moylesy does push it a bit.

There are downsides to having people around who are contractually obliged to laugh at you, though, and not just the potential for hospital trips. I, myself, came unstuck on one of my early jobs. I was doing the early breakfast show, so the newsreader and weather/traffic girl were in the studio with me – a more efficient way of having a 'posse' on a low-budget show. I was still quite new and although I had impressed all who came before me with my easy-going charm and vibrant-yet-crystal-clear diction, I still had nerves. It really hadn't been that long ago that I was standing in the middle of the geranium section addressing bemused geriatrics and here I was broadcasting to the nation. I firmly believe that there is no more beautiful sound than a woman laughing. There are, of course, notable exceptions, such as my mother, who sounds like a lawnmower running over Ian Brown of the Stone Roses singing unaccompanied.

Theresa was our girl doing the weather and travel and it's fair to say she was something of a looker. She was blonde with hazel eyes and her laugh was like a lawnmower running over Celine Dion singing with the London Philharmonic. She had one of those smiles that immediately puts you at ease and we had incredible chemistry. I wanted to impress her with every link, and it raised my game. Her laugh was addictive and, boy, was I hooked.

There's one instance I always remember. She was telling us about a traffic jam in the north-east of town. It was a well-to-do area and the perfect line popped into my head. She caught my eye and saw the glint in it. She paused to allow me to jump in in that perfect moment of understanding between two broadcasters coalescing as one. 'Are you sure it's a jam? I always thought they had traffic preserves up that way.' Boom. Her laugh erupted, the familiar Celine Dion singing 'Think Twice' (anyone who tells you that isn't her best is an idiot) and then the lawnmower hacked her to pieces. She could barely get through the rest of the report. I wanted to look away to make it easier for her to compose herself but I couldn't. Taking my eyes off her was a feat far, far beyond me.

I felt three feet taller with her in the room. It didn't make much difference because I was sitting down but I had so much confidence that I just threw out every link that came into my head. Puns, segues, innuendos, they flew out of me and every one landed.

When I was off sick and heard that same laugh following a mildly amusing but far from spectacular comment from my stand-in, it was like a dagger to the heart. I didn't think her a harlot, only a consummate professional. My wounded heart did take a while to heal but I'm just thankful I didn't declare my love or buy that diamond necklace I had put down a deposit on.

But I'm getting ahead of myself. I had just taken the call about standing in for Bruno Brookes. My hand trembled as I put the novelty banana phone back on its holster. I sat down and the room spun. I tried to compose myself and get my head in the right place mentally. I knew the systems they used and was confident that the more basic technical aspects like my faders would be OK. I'd spent so long practising that I would be able to do that without thinking. It was the links that I needed to get right. This was my chance to sell myself but I had no idea what I was going to say or do. I was paralysed in that moment and this was before I was even in the studio. I tried some basic vocal exercises but could manage little more than a squeak out of the back of my throat. It made me wonder if Joe Pasquale lives in a constant state of stage fright.

Unsurprisingly, I didn't sleep a wink that night and stared at the ceiling for hours. My voice began to come back which relaxed me a little and I was able to get through one or two of my vocal warm-ups: 'Duran Duran Do Daily Domino Discussions During Dynamic Dancing' and 'Adam Ant Always Amazes Aunts and Animals Amid ABBA Aerobics'. By 5.00am I was pretty confident that my voice was working but the show was in the afternoon so there was still a long time to be nervous.

My main concern was that I didn't have any life experience. Here I was – a twenty-year-old with plenty of enthusiasm but little to back it up. I thought about the Capital FM DJs who I'd listened to for hours and the times they talked about taking their kids to school or going to a wedding or having an amusing mishap while they put their bins out. As a fatherless wedding virgin who lived at home and took bin-emptying for granted, I simply couldn't do what they did. I thought about Terry, as I so often did. He had the longstanding joke where he referred to his utterly charming lifelong partner, Helen, as 'the current Mrs Wogan'. It wasn't just a brilliant joke but also a window into a life. It hints at experience, like a kindly uncle who reassures. I had no wife, I had nothing to say. How do I entertain the nation, keep them hooked? Why would they care what a twenty-year-old with astonishingly good hair has to say?

A car picked me up to take me to the studio. It was my dad's. He had taken the afternoon off work to run me down there. I appreciated the gesture but we still ended up arguing. 'Are you sure you can just take the afternoon off as a fireman?' I asked. He claimed to be angry about my tone and the fact that I was being ungrateful, but I think I'd hit a bit of a nerve and he was feeling pretty guilty. I was tactful the next morning and decided not to mention the article I saw in the paper about the inferno that had engulfed the shopping centre at the very same time that he was off on his little jaunt.

I don't remember anything about entering the building or reaching the studio. It was all a blur until the moment that the 'On Air' sign lit up and my fingers steadily and expertly raised the appropriate faders. I live for that red light. Suddenly, there was calm as I waited a half second before speaking. I love that half second. The air crackles with electricity and the world stops for a moment and you feel like you're going to explode with the potential that anything can happen in that moment. You'll often hear DJs, particularly the ones brought in because of their name rather than a background in radio broadcasting, finishing an off-mic conversation or saying that they're finishing a mouthful of tea when the mics go live. It seems to me that the idea is to create a casual vibe and a charming sense that they don't really know what they're doing. There are some broadcasters who hate this lack of professionalism with a passion and I understand that. Personally, I don't get angry about it – I just feel sorry for them because they're losing that magical half second which I think might be the best moment there is in the world.

It's easy to look at coincidences and decide that they are actually fate, so that's exactly what I'm going to do. The first record

I played was 'Favourite Shirts (Boy Meets Girl)' by none other than Haircut 100. As you can imagine, that made me really relax as I recalled the countless times strangers had shouted at me in the street to 'get a haircut'. It was a joke I'd always loved because, as I've said before, we all knew full well you just can't improve on perfection. All those anxieties about immaturity and lack of life experience did begin to climb up the back of my throat for the first link, though, and it was a strange sensation because I knew the blind panic was there but it was numbed by a serene calmness. So was I able to overcome my disadvantage? Did I somehow manage to speak to the people of the nation from my restrictively tender age?

'Good afternoon, everyone. My name's Pat and I'm here to play you some top tunes to get you that bit closer to home time. Not long to go, guys! Here's Haircut 100.'

Somehow, against all the odds, I did it.

In time, my confidence would grow and the next time I played the Haircut boys, I even worked in a bit of a gag intro-duction about how they're better than Haircut 99. The show went by in the blink of an eye but I was shaking with adrenalin when that 'On Air' light clicked off that fateful day.

I finished covering for Bruno and thought I'd done well. Despite that, I wasn't too surprised when they said thank you and goodbye at the end of the week. I knew there were no openings and it probably wasn't possible to do well enough to completely usurp Brookesy in five days. It didn't feel like the end when I walked out of those mystical doors, though. It felt like the beginning.

It's less the case these days, but the BBC opened a lot of doors for a young broadcaster. One of those doors led to Radio

Luxembourg. I was excited when they called. It was the sort of cool, semi-ironic name that screamed 'cutting edge' to me. I was slightly less excited when I realised that it was actually in Luxembourg. Still, I'd fully committed immediately and had no legal way of backing out even if I wanted to. I soon found out that it was the biggest commercial radio station in Europe with a really impressive history that is strongly linked to the pirate radio phenomena that shaped broadcasting in this country. I also found out that previous DJs included Noel Edmonds, Kenny Everett and Steve Wright. In subsequent years, that list included Chris Holmes, who would later be known by the surname Moyles. That's right, I'll put you out of your misery – Chris Moyles.

Things were going pretty well professionally but home life was still a bit tense. We would bicker, we would slam doors, we would huff and we would puff. Maybe the house was too small or maybe we just weren't sufficiently compatible to be seeing each other every day; but whatever it was, it seemed to go away when I decided to move out. I told my parents I was going in the middle of a huge row, so it was a complete and very pleasant surprise to find they both took the day off to help me. I thought it best not to question Dad's decision to take the time off and am pretty sure Mum still charged her client for that day. It was nice, though, and as I held them close after the last box was safely ensconced in my new little one-bedroom place, I just knew that everything was going to be OK. I was their beloved son again and they were the parents I cherished. We didn't speak again for seven years but sometimes, with the people you are most comfortable with, there is no need to speak. The fact that we went seven years speaks volumes about just how 'OK' things were with us.

I started throwing parties in my new 'Patchelor' pad and they became pretty wild affairs. Each time, I'd think that they would be relatively sedate but they would always spiral out of control. Inevitably, I would end up crawling into bed only two hours before I had to be up for work, sometimes with the party still going on in the small living room and kitchen. People would sometimes keep the good times going for another hour, or sometimes even until midnight. You're only young once.

Aunty Beeb had welcomed me back into her copious bosom and I was now doing the early breakfast show. The line between living the rock 'n' roll lifestyle of a DJ in his early twenties and being a functioning professional broadcaster is a difficult one to straddle, but straddle it I did. You don't get on the mic much in those early shows; those people unlucky enough to be awake either can't really focus on your words or just want music to try and get them through the unnatural existence of the nocturnal. It was good training because I knew the importance of being super upbeat on the occasions I did speak, even if I didn't feel like it. It's a skill I hold to this day and makes me the ideal funeral guest.

It's impossible to remember all of the things you talk about on the radio but there were a series of links that I'll always remember. I was talking about television and the three channels available at the time. I'd just finished playing Level 42 and had made a great joke about them being better than Level 41 when I uttered the famous adage: 'They say three's a crowd . . . but four's a party!' I'd been thinking about my successful bash the night before but went on to riff about how there should be another television channel – called 'The Fourth Channel'.

The reason I remember it is that I would later be at the launch party for Channel 4 and found myself talking to the founder. It was only when he said that he was an early riser that it clicked. I spoke about it a lot, he was up at the time I was broadcasting and, a few years later, we see that fourth channel suddenly appear. Admittedly, he'd gone with a slightly different name but it was too close to mine to be a coincidence.

Countdown was the first programme Channel 4 ever broadcast (a good one to note for pub quizzes) and I was very nearly the numbers guy (a good one to note for advanced pub quizzes). Not many people know that it came down to either me or Carol Vorderman for the job, which was how I came to be invited to the launch. She had an Oxbridge degree and an impressive, mathematical brain, I was good at pulling a suggestive face when somebody asked for 'a big one', so we both had quintessential skill sets for the job.

Carol got it in the end because I ended up missing my final screen test. I'd planned it all out – I left the house at 12.10pm and it was an eighteen-minute walk to the bus stop for a bus that was due in twenty-one minutes. The bus took forty-three minutes and there was an eleven-minute walk at the other end. By the time I got there for my 12.30pm appointment, Carol had already been given the job. I still don't really know what went wrong; these things are usually political, but it's such a shame because I know I would have been brilliant. I would just have to be brilliant doing something else.

Chapter 4

Scatman John – 'Scatman (Ski-Ba-Bop-Ba-Dop-Bop)'

We all have those songs that we encounter at an impressionable age that we feel were written specifically for us. I can't help but feel a bit creeped out about how much these lyrics speak to me.

The past is a foreign country – there are opportunities there. Sydney has its opera house, Munich has the Gasteig Concert Hall, Vienna presumably has an impressive music building of some description and the BBC has Studio A on Dickenson Road in Rusholme, Manchester. Actually, they may not any more, but they did when *Top of the Pops* started. Elstree, that leafy village in beautiful Hertfordshire, is probably more famous than Rusholme for its studios. And in those studios (handily named Elstree Studios), *Top of the Pops* was filmed when it, sadly, like we all must sooner or later, ended.

It has been over a decade since *TOTP* (this is a handy abbreviation I will use to save time and make things easier when referring to *Top of the Pops* from here on in. It should save a lot of space, too, only using the initial letters T–O–T–P rather than laboriously writing out the full words 'Top of the Pops' every time. That's the thing with these books – when you've got a whole life to fit in, you need to be mindful of space and don't have time to be writing *Top of the Pops* every time. So to recap: *TOTP* is *Top of the Pops*) ended.

TOTP aired its final episode in 2006. I was honoured to be asked to come back and co-host the show alongside some of the greats who have chatted their way through the charts. It was my first appearance since the early '80s but it is undeniable that my reign hosting the nation's favourite pop music show, which began in 1982, lasted the best part of a quarter of a century. Sure, there was a pretty big gap between 1983 and that final appearance in 2006, but I like to think of myself as the Sir Alex Ferguson of presenting music chart television programmes. We are both noted for lengthy reigns characterised by longevity, success and putting faith in the youth. Plus we both like chewing gum.

If there is a heaven, it will look a little like *TOTP* (there's that abbreviation again – told you it would make things easier). As a kid, I would revel in experiencing these voices that I knew so well from the radio come out of actual human heads. The thing that the producers of the show realised that so many others failed to comprehend is that it isn't about the music. Sure, the programme consisted of performances from some of the week's best-selling popular music artists but there was a reason they were, more often than not, asked to mime. Whether they realised it or not, people were in it for the presenters, as they skilfully elicited just enough enthusiasm from the crowd for each act to come across well on telly but not so much that they overwhelmed the musicians. I know it's a cliché, but just thinking about Tony Blackburn saying, 'Here's The Beatles with "I Want to Hold Your Hand",' gives me goosebumps to this day. It actually upsets me to hear that song because I'll always have to listen to it without the lift that Tony gives it. Unless I'm watching *TOTP2* (that's an abbreviation for *Top of the Pops 2*; you'll notice that it works in much the same way as the other handy abbreviation I introduced. We are absolutely decimating this word count).

When youngsters these days ask me how to break into television, I am usually more than a little surprised but hugely touched. There is no one right way to get on the box so all I can do is tell my story because that's what worked for me. It all started with an innocuous comment from my then boss, a man who we'll call Tony Benali (primarily because that's his name).

'Patman, you know you really don't have a face for radio.'

I was baffled. Not by the 'Patman' bit – everyone at Radio 1 called me that. I was originally christened 'Patman Do' as a nod to the fact that I'd *do* just about anything to get a laugh on air and had once been to Nepal. This had morphed into Patman over time and I had no problems with that at all. But 'not having a face for radio' seemed a little harsh from a man I considered a friend. I was still a petulant young man so decided to do the sensible thing and count to ten before replying.

'What the fuck's that supposed to mean?'

'Well, you're a good-looking fella . . . you should be on the telly, too.'

I can't remember ever having felt so embarrassed. Having a face for radio was something you heard a lot around the BBC and I'd always just assumed it was a compliment meaning someone fitted in nicely. Now I knew why Annie Nightingale gave me a wide berth in the canteen. How many first dates had I inadvertently ruined? And charity trips to visit children in hospital? It didn't bear thinking about. Having a face for radio was a bad thing. Not having a face for radio was a good thing. I thanked Tony and apologised profusely once I'd taken this all in but, by that stage, he was long gone.

I began to think about TV more and more and realised that, if I had a face for anything, it might just be that. The transition from radio wouldn't be easy but I felt like I just needed an opportunity to prove myself. Fortunately, the BBC had a scouting system in those days. Unfortunately, it was second to most.

Most people don't know that the BBC had a scouting system in the early '80s similar to that used by football clubs up and down the country. It is important that talent should never slip through the net, so the idea is that everyone gets seen. Word got around that *TOTP* was looking for young blood and that a scout could rock up during the recording of any BBC radio show. I was so nervous around that time that I almost forgot to use conditioner on the seventh phase of my morning wash. This scout could come at any moment and I probably wouldn't even know he was there. I would just have to bring my A+ game (for when A just isn't enough) every single day and hope for the best.

After a couple of weeks of this, I started to think they'd never send anyone to see me and, I admit, my game probably teetered somewhere around the A-/B+ stage. One morning, I rocked up at work and entered the studio a few minutes before I was due to go on air. I nodded hello to the usual suspects. Then I spotted a bald gentleman with glasses sitting in the corner of our tiny booth holding a pen and a pad of paper. He wasn't Jeremy the continuity announcer; he wasn't Susan who read the news. Something told me this might just be it.

I tried to focus on what I did best and not let the occasion overwhelm me. It was crucial to consider this a normal show, like any other. I made a terrific joke about The Jackson 5 being so much better than The Jackson 4 and I'm fairly sure I saw a smile flicker across the scout's face. It was an exemplary bit of banter and we all knew it. He left without a word at the end of the show but a letter arrived chez Pat by the end of the week informing me that, subject to a screen test, I was the next presenter of *Top of the Pops* (they didn't use the abbreviation so neither will I on this occasion).

The screen test was equally terrifying. To avoid a repetition of my *Countdown* error, my driver picked me up and got me to Elstree in good time and I'm still very grateful to Dad for that. Eagle-eyed readers might recall that I mentioned earlier that I didn't speak to my parents for seven years but who said anything about speaking? This was far from a Miss Daisy dynamic and my old man was good enough to let me focus in total silence.

While I was concerned that Dad might hum en route or that he might talk and ruin how clearly OK we were with each other, that was nothing compared to my worries upon entering the building. Radio was all I knew so I asked a passer-by in the lobby where the equipment was kept and headed there directly. An hour later, the executive producer of *TOTP* found me in the control room amidst a sea of wires and patiently explained that television was different. I would have to cede some control and get back to my first love – presenting.

The main difference between being on camera and being off it is the cameras. This might sound obvious but I cannot tell you how many times that day a voice in my earpiece uttered the words, 'You're picking your nose again, Pat.'

Miming was another issue. It was a well-known fact that those appearing on *TOTP* were asked to mime but nobody bothered to tell muggins here that presenters had to do it live. 'All of the work and none of the credit' just about sums it up. I'm a fast learner and sensed what they wanted. I removed the finger from my nostril and spoke at an audible volume. I could see they were blown away but the producer of the show was ever the professional and tempered his praise somewhat.

'Not great. Obviously the hair's amazing but you definitely need to do a bit more work outside the radio studio before we'll have you on.'

I was buzzing. It was clear that I was destined for BBC One.

I read between the lines and realised I needed to do a bit more work outside the radio studio before they'd have me on. I had a word with the powers that be and convinced them to let me have a crack at some outside broadcasts. They weren't convinced at first but I told them I had something they might want and we reached an agreement. Within a few weeks, my Radio 1 show was being broadcast live from Brent Cross shopping centre and they knew the secret to good grooming was combing counter-clockwise.

If we were going to do the show in a crowded space, it was important it was good. I knew the big dogs at the Beeb weren't entirely convinced by the whole venture and that I'd need to give them something bold, something innovative, something utterly transformative. I thought long and hard and came up with an idea that still ranks in my all-time top seven – a talent show.

I was no longer simply introducing songs and playing music; I was doing the thing I had dreamed of all my life – introducing people. I was finally riffing with the general public and I couldn't have been happier. Sure, there was the odd crying baby and the occasional fan who wanted to touch the hair but that's part and parcel of fame. Another innovation of mine was the idea that people could call in and request songs they wanted to hear. You'll be unsurprised to hear the phone didn't stop ringing in those early days – some things definitely change.

The talent show aspect was the real draw, however. It had come to me while walking the dog on Hampstead Heath one afternoon. I was mentally compiling a list of all the things I loved. These included magic, music, comedy, origami and the smell of freshly cut grass. Then it hit me like freefalling gunge – how about a talent show? OK, it might be difficult to incorporate origami and grass but, as Meat Loaf so nearly sang, three out of five ain't bad. Carol may have got the *Countdown* job but even I know that works out as 60 per cent of my passions covered.

There were teething problems, there always are. This was radio and I'm the first to admit that the mime acts simply didn't work. Actually, I was about the fifth to admit that but I got there in the end.

To this day, I can still remember an eight-year-old boy who well and truly floored me with a magic trick. My producer insisted that, like the seemingly endless parade of mime artists, this simply did not work on radio. I disagreed and maintain that my reactions made for compelling radio. 'What an incredible sleight of hand,' I said . . . 'No way!' I gasped . . . 'I have never been so simultaneously excited and fearful of sorcery,' I squealed . . . but apparently that wasn't enough. Perhaps I should have been more critical; it can't have escaped your notice that Simon Cowell took my talent show idea and gave it a negative bent a few years later and it became a global phenomenon. Being critical just isn't my jam.

Doing those outside broadcasts really helped me hone my style and gave me the confidence I needed but there was still something missing. I decided a retreat was the answer. If I could get away for a few days and sort my head out then there was no question that they'd have me on the telly before too long. I knew I had to go somewhere with maximum pun potential for on-air humour once I got back (puns just feel better when there's truth behind them) but Jamaica was out because I've never really been one for lounging around in the sun and I didn't know where Jakarta was so didn't fancy that either. I decided on a wonderful country in Scandinavia enabling me to use solid material upon my return like: 'Me? Go on holiday? No(r)way!' Obviously, I pronounced the 'r' but the joke works better on paper using brackets.

What an incredible country Norway is. Wikipedia, some kind of online travel guide, simply doesn't do it justice: 'It has a total area of 385,252 sq km (148,747 sq mi) and a population of 5,109,059 people (2014) . . . The country shares a long eastern border with Sweden (1,619 km or 1,006 mi long). Norway is bordered by Finland and Russia to the north-east, and the Skagerrak Strait to the south, with Denmark on the other side. Norway has an extensive coastline, facing the North Atlantic Ocean and the Barents Sea.'

It's remarkable to me that the website can list topic after topic, from biodiversity to union with Sweden, and fail to mention the country's greatest contribution to history – the mullet.

I am often credited with popularising the hairstyle in this country but, much like *Fun House*, it was an idea pilfered from abroad. I noticed that so many Viking Norwegian men had the look and knew it was the one for me. The great thing about the mullet, beyond the fact that the ladies can't get enough of it, is that it's all business at the front and all party at the back. Until now, my magnificent hair had been the finest marble known to man. Finally, Michelangelo had come along to sculpt it into an absolute masterpiece. (That's just a metaphor; my hairdresser's name is Trevor and my hair is actually made of hair.)

By the time I returned to England, I had everything I needed – confidence, experience, fashion sense and a wife. And, most importantly of all, I had the hairstyle that I knew would make me stand out from the crowd.

Finally, I was ready for *Top of the Pops* (written out fully again here for dramatic effect).

Chapter 5

Pet Shop Boys – 'Always on my Mind'

For me this is Neil and Chris, The Pat Sharp Boys, at their very best. I don't think there can be a higher compliment for this song than the one and only Elvis Presley choosing to cover it.

'Fame lulls the fever of the soul and makes us feel that we have grasped an immortality.' So wrote the American poet Joaquin Miller, although the whole immortality thing was undermined somewhat when he died in 1913. As ever, pop (in the form of Irene Cara in this case) put it better: 'Fame – I'm gonna make it to heaven.' I really hope I make it to heaven (or, as I prefer to think of it, that great Fun House in the sky. Hopefully, God will let me guest host occasionally).

It's interesting that you can split my celebrity chums into two groups; there are those who remember one defining moment when they were suddenly famous. They had one moment, one key moment that grabbed them from obscurity and held them up to the sun of fame like Rafiki does to Simba in *The Lion King*. For others, their career gradually developed and fame did so at the same pace until, one day, they stopped and looked around and thought 'Hey, I'm famous.'

I'm in the second category. *TOTP* was obviously a huge break and put my face into the homes of millions of people, but it wasn't quite like Michael Owen scoring against Argentina in the 1998 World Cup or Prince George being born. For them, there is the one moment everyone remembers when they entered the public consciousness and often it's quite sad that the celebrities in this category fail to surpass that instance when they arrived on the fairground of fame. Michael Owen had a decent career but it never quite matched the dizzying heights of that goal. As for Prince George, since being born he's not achieved a great deal (at the time of writing). Sure, he's done some good work wearing some natty outfits but I'm told by a reliable source that he has someone to pick them out for him.

You could say my name is pretty synonymous with *Fun House* but, obviously, I was famous before that, and, less obviously, after. I like being in the group that slowly became famous. For one thing, it's easier to deal with (more on that in a bit) but I also find it more interesting. One of my favourite conversations with other famous folk in this category is discussing the moment when it dawns on people that they're famous because it's always different. Often, it's quite insignificant, but if you ask Jasper Carrott or Cat Deeley or Timothy Spall then they will all be able to remember one specific moment of clarity when they thought, 'I'm a legit famous person.' It may be seeing your name as a crossword clue (Deeley); being given a meal in a Chinese restaurant on the house (Carrott); or finding that your divorce is being covered by a local newspaper (Spall).

Personally, I actually had a couple of false alarms. I often forget just how young I was when I made my first dalliance with the spotlight. When you're only just out of your teens, you feel like the world is your oyster. I suppose it is in many ways. It's hard to crack for some, easy for others and its contents make some people horny and others sick. The first time I walked out of Bruno Brookes's studio, I expected to be stopped for autographs. Then when I walked out of the *TOTP* studio after my first show hosting, I thought there would be girls desperate for my attention at the back door. To be fair, there were girls there, but they were waiting for Shakin' Stevens. I took it pretty badly at the time. I pushed my way through the crowd, trying to catch the eye of a fan who might want to thrust their sparkly pad and equally sparkly pen in my direction, but to no avail. I loitered on the fringes of the crowd and my arrogance and expectation slowly slipped into self-pity and desperation. Just one signature. If I was asked for just one signature, then I would go home happy.

Shakin' came out and got a raucous reception from the crowd who made a mockery of my assumption that they couldn't get any louder. The crowd thinned but found its voice again when Heaven 17 came out. There were only a handful by the time The Flying Pickets emerged, but they were rewarded for the patience with photos and some genial chatter. Brian Hibbard ducked back inside to get his hat and the rest of the band drifted off, taking the last of the autograph hunters with them. By the time Brian came back, I was the only one left standing outside. I was leaning against a bin that I would later find out left an unidentifiable brown stain on my stonewashed jeans and I was staring at an unremarkable spot on the ground. I looked up when I felt Brian's hand on my shoulder. 'Your time will come, mate. Now get yourself home.' He popped his hat on his head and whistled as he walked away. I have never heard whistling like it.

His words reassured me but I still felt hurt and ashamed. I was angry that none of those people wanted my autograph and I was angry at myself for being angry. It's like when people say the more depressed they feel, the more they eat and the more they eat, the more depressed they feel. It's a vicious circle. Although how vicious can something involving cake really be? Maybe it's different if you don't like cake. Anyway, it was a valuable lesson and I turned my attention to my craft rather than the by-products of it.

It's no secret that the famous are treated differently to other members of society. The great irony that these wealthy stars get freebies and preferential treatment at the time they no longer need them is one of my conversational set pieces at dinner parties. It never fails to get general nods and murmurs of agreement. Never.

I would be lying if I didn't say that I've benefited from the odd showbusiness sampler or B-lister benefit and I'm ashamed to say that there have been parts of me that have exhibited a sense of entitlement. That's not to say that I ever barge into places and say, 'Do you know who I am?' (unless visiting an elderly relative in an assisted care home). I've never expected to be given anything but, on the occasions that a meal has been comped or I get some new trainers, I have thought that I deserve them for my services to the people of this country and, to a lesser extent, the people of Europe and, to an even lesser extent, the people of America and Canada. I remember on one occasion I received three identical pairs of high-end trainers. I thought nothing of having one pair at home, one pair that I kept in a suitcase for trips and a third pair to keep pens in. Nowadays, I'd obviously share the wealth and find a better use for them, although it doesn't really happen any more. I am, however, more than open to receiving just about anything you might wish to send me.

My ego was very welcomingly punctured by that exchange at the doors to the *TOTP* studio but there were still occasions when it got the better of me. As I said, my rise to fame was a slow and steady one and not particularly easy to chart. One measure would be becoming aware of people looking at you and whispering to each other but – and I don't want to sound vain here – I was used to that happening. With hair like mine, people notice you. I'm a decent-looking guy but I'm under no illusions that it's the hair that people notice.

Even before my time in Auntie's bosom (the BBC, not Auntie Dot), I could sense heads turning when I walked into a room. I would hear smatterings of 'unbelievable volume' . . . 'it's a masterpiece' . . . or 'I'm leaving you, Helen. I've found a new love.'

So I think that made it even more difficult to be aware of my growing fame. A few times I thought that I'd had my 'cross-word' moment. One was when I was going for lunch at quite a nice hotel out in the country for Auntie's birthday (Auntie Dot, not the BBC). Her side of the family had the money so it was a fancy place. I rolled up in my Vauxhall Nova and a well-dressed guy came running out and offered to park my car for me. I relinquished control of the Patmobile and made a right royal fool of myself inside when I made claims to all and sundry that the complimentary valet parking service was in some way unique to me.

Another was when I went into my regular coffee shop and they refused to accept any money for my cappuccino with extra chocolate sprinkles. Brimming with hubris, I went back the next day for another and didn't even bother taking out my wallet. I was told in no uncertain terms that because, on this occasion, I hadn't already paid for six coffees, I could not have the free seventh. In a rather undignified manner, I tried to negotiate having the first one free and then paying for coffees two through seven, but management were unwavering.

I'm sure there are further examples but the only other one that comes to mind was my own Deeley-esque crossword moment. I was reading over somebody's shoulder on a train and saw that they had pencilled in 'Sharp' for 13 across. I scooped the paper off their seat when they left only to read the heart-breaking clue: '13 across – not blunt (5)'. One day I would have my crossword moment, but it would be several years later. I was doing the crossword myself and I thought about Brian Hibbard and his wonderful whistling and warm hand.

One sign of my burgeoning fame was when I got to meet Diana, Princess of Wales, during a luncheon to launch Capital Radio's Help a London Child charity appeal (see pictures). I stood next to Nigel Havers as Sir Richard Attenborough and the Princess made their way down the line and spoke with us each in turn. It's very daunting to speak to an angel in human form since it can be extremely difficult to find common ground. The one thing I had realised in advance was that we'd both had ups and downs in our relationships, something that's entirely natural in the glare of the spotlight. I explained to her that it sometimes felt as though the mullet got so much attention that 'there were three of us in this marriage, so it was a bit crowded'. I thought nothing more of the remark until I saw Diana use it, verbatim, in her *Panorama* interview with Martin Bashir a few years later. To this day, I still don't understand why she said it as neither she nor Charles had ever sported a mullet to the best of my knowledge.

So what was my free meal, crossword clue, unwelcome local paper coverage moment? When did I realise that I was a proper famous person? It was an invitation. Noel Edmonds was already a household name when I was earning my spotlight stripes. I had been an admirer of his radio work for some time and thought he was a gifted *TOTP* presenter, too. *The Multi-Coloured Swap Shop* was one of the biggest hits on television at the time and really cemented him as the real deal on the box. It's a real shame they were never able to sell the rights to America since Noel was such a stickler for the English spelling and 'Colored' simply wasn't going to cut it. I walked past him in Auntie's corridor a couple of times (both) and he had that swagger, that presence.

Almost as soon as I began edging my way into BBC circles, I heard about Noel's prominent place in the social hierarchy. Once every couple of months or so, the whispers would begin. People would talk excitedly and hopefully about an upcoming event. Noel would be opening his doors for one of the greatest get-togethers in history. The whole building would go quiet when Noel arrived, head held high and clutching an armful of golden envelopes. It was like the Algonquin Round Table but better – Kenny Everett was there.

I knew that I'd turned the corner into Fame Street when I saw this entrance for the eighth time. 'Patman . . .' He gave me a wink and, more significantly, an envelope. In the most beautiful calligraphy, it bore my name – Patman Sharp. I wondered if he had mistaken my often-used nickname for my actual name but could make peace with that. I had made the inner circle – I was going to one of Noel Edmonds's famed Home Gatherings™.

The invitations were issued only three days before the event so I didn't have too long to get anxious, which was a blessing. It meant that I only had seven standing hair appointments to get ready but thankfully the humidity was kind and I was able to be near the top of my game when it was time to lift the huge knocker on Noel's front door. It was a lion but had been modified slightly to bear Noel's face.

His home was breathtaking; everything was marble and grand and vast. There were no decorations specific to the occasion but everything was spotless. Interestingly, there were more 270v razor plug sockets than regular electric sockets. It meant that Noel was never more than 10ft from being able to plug in an electric razor, which goes some way to explaining his impeccably-kept beard.

I know you'll want to hear an exhaustive list of the stars in attendance but, regrettably, alcohol (others) and adrenalin (me) were flowing and have clouded things somewhat. That's not to say the memory cupboard is entirely bare. It would be impossible to forget Russell Grant, for instance. I'm a big fan of his larger-than-life persona and it was a great joy to hear his laugh reverberating beneath Noel's high ceilings. It became louder as the evening went on and Russell threw himself into the heart of proceedings. He told me in the least secretive voice I'd ever heard that discussions were in place to make some kind of televised version of Noel's Home Gathering™ and, as you are surely aware, those discussions went well with the slight exception of Noel refusing to relinquish his rights to the name that he had trademarked.

After the dessert trolley came round, Russell told me that Noel wanted to have a sidekick. It made sense to have a boisterous, funny and lively character to play foil to Noel's measured and professional demeanour. Russell was extremely excited about the prospect and got a bit carried away. He had come up with a couple of name ideas like 'Mr Booby' and 'Mr Robby'. I can still see him bounding around the house in his bright polka-dot-shirt-and-trouser combo, speaking in his excited, high-pitched voice and often falling over. A rotund figure sporting a pink shirt adorned with yellow spots, Granty constantly repeated the same gibberish phrases ad infinitum all evening. Russell once said to me that he was told that he needed to audition as a formality for legal reasons and yet he never did get that sidekick role. Apparently, Noel muttered something about TV executives but that doesn't sound right because I know Noel was one of the executives. Noel and Russell don't speak any longer, which is a real shame.

There was an excited and giddy air throughout the whole house. We played a number of games, the first of which was Spin the Bottle. I'd never played before – a side-effect of spending my time perfecting my craft rather than living out a more 'normal' social development in my teens. I was a bit nervous to begin with but everyone was friendly and I was soon able to laugh along with everyone else. I found it genuinely exhilarating watching that bottle spin. The noise of the crowd would build as the bottle gradually lost its momentum and there would be an eruption of whooping and laughing as the glass neck settled in the direction of one of the players. We played for a solid hour and people's enthusiasm didn't wane in the slightest. Then Anne Diamond chipped in with a suggestion – she thought it might add a little spice if the person who the bottle pointed to had to kiss the person who had spun it. Having a bottle pointing at you was one thing, but then having to kiss someone at random? I made my excuses and went over to the kitchen.

I was just in time for a game of pass the parcel. It was a lot of fun although it was pretty irritating whenever Chris Tarrant had the parcel. Most people would rip the layer of wrapping paper off immediately to see if the sweet prize inside was to be theirs, but he would be extremely ponderous. He'd loudly ask rhetorical questions and unnecessarily drag things out. 'Let's see . . . is this the last layer of paper? Have I won the prize? We'll find out . . . after this break . . .' He would then go to the toilet or get some more Twiglets or something and then come back. I lost patience in the end so don't know who won or even what the prize was.

As a side note, I got in trouble with Chris years later when he invited me to a recording of a quiz show he was hosting and I brought with me a packet of jelly babies. I've always loved throwing sweets into the air and catching them in my mouth but it seemed, on that fateful day in 2001, that they kept going down the wrong hole and causing me to cough. It was probably annoying for the people at the recording but there was no harm done, and I don't think it had any lasting impact.

You will have noticed, as I did, that the games we played at those parties were all pretty juvenile. Although there was alcohol, adult-themed conversation and even some amorous canoodling, the gathering did feel a bit like a children's party. I think you can attribute that to two things. First, fame encourages arrested development. As the 'talent', you're surrounded by people whose job it is to remove as much responsibility from you as possible. The 'talent' needs not to be burdened by tasks or chores or admin or thinking or planning or consequences. In that respect, it's like being a child, so it makes sense for celebrities either not to grow up or revert back to a childlike state. I'm sure he won't mind me telling you this, but Tim Vincent of *Blue Peter* fame still eats rusks. He says that he just likes the way that they're big salty biscuits and he does have a point. You could say that this is simply another case of youth being wasted on the young, but I think it would be foolish to completely discount the possibility that Tim Vincent still has, at least in a nominal way, the mind of a small child.

The second thing is that a lot of the people at the party worked in kids' TV; *Multi-Coloured Swap Shop, Tiswas, TOTP* and more were all represented at that party by their respective hosts. One of the golden rules of presenting a kids' show is to talk to the audience at their level, but you cannot be patronising. Personally, I don't think that it's something you can teach. It's something you definitely get better at but it's still kind of instinctive. Most of the people at that party spent more time talking to callers, participants or audience members who were under eighteen, which meant they were bound to find their personalities reflecting that.

I definitely think there's something in it. Especially after I went to that war correspondents' party and everybody spoke in sombre tones over the nibbles. I'll never forget John Simpson talking about the joy of the birth of his first child with a furrowed brow and respectfully downbeat tone. Haunting.

I wasn't the first to leave the party but I definitely did not want to be the last. For some reason, Chris Tarrant was in charge of the goody bags by the door. It took me literally three-quarters of an hour to get out of the house. A small queue formed that became longer and longer because every time Chris went to hand over the bag, he would retract it at the last second and squeak, 'But we don't want to give you that . . .' It was extremely annoying and a lot of people gave up waiting. Was it worth hanging around that long for a packet of Parma Violets, a couple of balloons and a cheap yo-yo? Probably not, but it at least gave me the chance to tell Chris to stop his annoying behaviour. These irritating quirks would only hold him back and keep him away from primetime entertainment, which I knew was his ambition.

I was buzzing on the way home from the party; so much so that I walked the whole way. It hadn't been quite what I had expected but it was still intoxicating to be in the presence of so many high-profile celebs and bottles of vodka. It was towards the end of that walk that I developed my kids' TV theory to explain the behaviour. I loved those presenters and respected the hell out of them, but I knew that it wasn't exactly what I wanted to do. Kids' TV – not for me. No way. Absolutely not. No chance. Never.

Chapter 6

Madness – 'House of Fun'

I like this for obvious reasons.

L ife was pretty good. It's a lovely feeling to wake up excited about the day ahead of you – to grin as you pull back the curtains, to beam as you walk into your bathroom, to smile as you slide into the kitchen in your socks, to laugh as you collect your post from the doormat. Everything just felt right, I was king of my manor and everything felt so positive. I think it's so important to have that sanctuary – especially when your time isn't always your own out in the big wide world.

'Fame, fame, fatal fame – it can play hideous tricks on the brain.' So sang Morrissey Smith in 'Frankly, Mr Shankley' but I suspect he'd have cheered up a bit if he'd got a burger down him once in a while. I've had that musing about big M's diet for years but I was never able to use it at the time because that song was never released as a single. Still, it's difficult to deny it's a cracking chapter opener and just goes to show that if you have a good idea, however seemingly insignificant, you must always write it down.

Another relevant song is 'A Day in the Life' by The Beatles (apart from all that weird stuff about Blackburn, Lancashire). As a famous person, one of the things I've been most often asked is, 'What is a typical day like?' Well, I can go along with the bit where John and Paul sang, 'Woke up, fell out of bed . . .' but after that things fall apart somewhat. 'Dragged a comb across my head . . .' – I mean, really? It's little wonder that, when it comes to hair, I'm far more of a respected figure than any of the Fab Four. With my collaborator in pop, I also released five singles that made the Top 75 but it's probably fair to say most people know more of The Beatles' music than mine. I think both the boys and I will take a 1–1 draw.

As a celebrity, there is no such thing as a typical day. There are days when Madonna has to squeeze into some kind of ridiculous outfit and gyrate with some young male dancers but other days she'll record a music video or do a gig. Sometimes, Sting plays a gig in a football stadium but on others spends so long in the bath that Trudie jokes that he looks like a prune. That's life. All I can do is talk you through the kind of day that wasn't untypical at the height of my early fame. You've got a good sense of what a working day consisted of so here's a stab at a 'day off'. While it is quite possible not all of these things really happened on one particular day, they give you a flavour of life just about in sight of the top:

7.00am – I am woken by the sound of my clock radio. Although his wife and immediate neighbours might beg to differ, it is absolutely essential that the first thing one hears in the morning is the voice of Mike Read. Hit the snooze button.

7.10am – Get out of bed and carefully remove hairnet.

7.15am — Head to the bathroom to prepare myself and my hair for the coming day. Do the first wee of the day standing up.

9.30am — Exit bathroom to allow hairspray fumes to dissipate.

9.40am — Re-enter bathroom to finish hair.

10.35am — Put on denim jacket with matching denim jeans. Ensure gold medallion and chest hair are perfectly aligned.

10.45am — In many ways, I imagine nothing has changed for the younger generation of radio presenters. The first thing I always did upon leaving my bedroom was to check the fax machine and no doubt it's much the same for Greg James.

11.00am — Go through the post and answer any fan mail.

2.00pm — Time for lunch. This could vary but would most commonly feature cheese on sticks, pineapple on sticks and sausages on sticks (we preferred to eat stuff on sticks rather than take selfies with them back in the '80s). Wall's Viennetta optional for pudding. Normally the classic blue one.

3.00pm — Step into the Patmobile and head to the hospital for a spot of mingling with some fans. Every so often, I'm introduced to some poor blighter who's lost his hair and am told that friends and family are shaving theirs off as a sign of solidarity. Obviously, that's out of the question for me but I always offer to trim my chest hair. My suggestion tends to be declined.

5.00pm – Back home and it's time to unwind after a difficult after-noon. If I'm alone, I can while away hours playing with my Speak and Spell, Spirograph and Etch A Sketch. You might think that's childish but no less an authority than Neil Buchanan once said my sketching using the latter device called to mind Monet in his later work. I would eventually learn that Monet was blind by the end and didn't speak to Neil for a year and a half. In truth, I'm not sure our relationship has ever fully recovered.

6.00pm – Off to the hairdresser (not the barber; never the barber). This can be awkward because it's difficult for Glenda to ask how my holidays were when she sees me three times a week. At least the lack of small-talk means she can focus on the job in hand and give it her fullest attention.

9.30pm – Head to Wimpy for dinner or eat a meal at home consisting of prawn cocktail, steak garni and Black Forest Gâteau. Sign auto-graphs for adoring fans while waiting for the food to arrive if out.

10.30pm – Nightly ablutions performed, it's time for my beauty sleep. Plenty of people have told me it doesn't look like I need a great deal but, trust me, I'm not myself unless I get the full eight-and-a-half hours.

As you can see, even days off when you're famous feel a lot like days on. But what about today? Has anything really changed? Allow me to talk you through it:

7.00am – I am woken by the sound of my clock radio. Although his wife might beg to differ, it is absolutely essential that the first thing one hears in the morning is the voice of Nick Grimshaw. Do not hit the snooze button, time is precious.

7.10am – Get out of bed and carefully remove hairnet.

7.15am – Head to the bathroom to prepare myself and my hair for the coming day. Do the first wee of the day sitting down.

11.00am – Exit bathroom. You will notice that took longer than it did in the first flush of youth. Also that I've developed an immunity to aerosol spray.

11.05am – Time to get dressed. Obviously I no longer go with double denim; times have changed and I've changed with them. Usually I opt for something simple like flared jeans and a black leather jacket. Welcome to the noughties! Or, as I prefer to think of them, naughties. [N.B. This joke won't work as well on the audiobook.]

11.15am – Go through the post and answer any fan mail.

11.20am – Give serious consideration to getting a new credit card.

11.21am – Call my agent and see what's come in.

11.25am – While away a few minutes on Twitter.

1.00pm – Lunch. This can vary but usually involves salad. I like to pretend that I'm eating cheese on sticks. Sometimes, I'll even use a toothpick and thread it through the lettuce but it doesn't really help.

2.00pm – Step into the Patmobile and head to the hospital for a spot of mingling with some fans. Bit of hassle, actually, being allowed in the building. The kids seem to have some trouble placing me and more often than not I'm referred to as 'Mrs'. Still, if I put a smile on one face then it's been a good afternoon. There aren't that many good afternoons.

4.00pm – Back home and it's time to unwind after a difficult afternoon. I'm not one to live in the past so obviously I no longer play with 1980s toys. These days I'm an avid gamer and have almost completed Donkey Kong Country on the Super Nintendo. I once said in company that men are like Super Nintendo games – they work better if you blow them. (Dust would collect in the bottom of the cartridge and nine times out of ten they wouldn't work first time and you'd have to dislodge the detritus with your breath. We had it tough back in the day. You never get this with Candy Crush.) I thought it was a great line but it didn't go down all that well. That's the thing about television awards ceremonies – there aren't that many computer game fans present.

5.00pm – Off to the hairdresser (not the barber; never the barber). Glenda has ceased trying small-talk but her abilities with the scissors are undiminished with the passing of time. Without me, her kids wouldn't have been able to go to university. I feel a sense of pride about that.

8.30pm – Dinner at home. If I went out, it's possible I'd have to sign stuff all night. Autographs, photos, breasts. Once you reach a certain age, the appeal of having these thrust in your face wears off. We can never know for sure that I'd be bombarded, but it is possible. Often, I will ask my wife to make the kinds of things I used to eat at Wimpy. It's never quite the same.

10.30pm – Nightly ablutions performed, it's time for my beauty sleep. I don't sleep as soundly as I used to and when I dream I dream of regular work. It feels so real at the time and then I wake up in a cold sweat. They say you can never go back and, sadly, they are right.

Chapter 7

Edwin Starr – 'War'

A poignant reminder of the futility of war and of Shadow's fierce dominance with the pugil stick on Gladiators.

It's a great honour to get to entertain the country and it's also a great honour to fight for it. So to do both is an honour squared. I achieved honour to the power of two back in the '80s and it's a memory that has stayed with me.

I think it's easy to become a bit cynical about supporting the troops with all the whooping and hollering that the Americans do. Whenever I watch a bit of WWE wrestling, there seems to be a bit about them going over to do shows for the armed forces and it all looks like pomp and ceremony, but it really does make a difference and there's a special bond you feel with those young people. Whenever I watch a crowd of troops cheer as Mick Foley jumps 30ft from a steel cage through a pile of tables, I'm reminded that I brought the same joy when I pressed a button to play The Human League.

When my agent told me that the armed forces were interested, I jumped at the chance (he snuck up behind me and shouted the news in my ear). Perhaps it was naivety, but I didn't for one second think about the potential dangers. Maybe it was because of my age – when you're in your twenties you feel bulletproof – or maybe it was because I was so focused on doing what felt like my national duty that there was no space for anxiety or terror. It's also possible that I knew that my posting in Tenerife was unlikely to be particularly perilous.

Having said that, things were a bit hairier than I had anticipated (an awful lot of French on those beaches). The original plan was for me to get a boat to a nearby base and be choppered in from there but the army gentleman that I was making arrangements with would not budge on the rule about me having to wear a helmet. Obviously, that was an absolute deal breaker for me, especially with gigs coming up. It's no exaggeration to say that, for me, helmet hair is the injury equivalent of a professional football player breaking his leg in six places. Possibly worse.

I needed to pay for my own flights, but I was happy to do so. Flying was much easier for me back then. There were no limits on liquids in your hand luggage or even sharp objects so I could fill my rucksack with scissors, clippers, tweezers, mousses, serums, gels, waxes, gums, creams and everything else I needed to combat the dry air of a pressurised cabin. The conditions weren't ideal for me but I could cope. Some say that the 100ml liquid limits and restrictions on sharp objects is a small price to pay for being and feeling safe. I say it's a huge price to pay. Is it worth paying? Arguably, yes. But still.

There was nobody to meet me at the airport, which worried me. I wasn't worried for me but how can the forces win a war if they can't get such basic logistics correct? I may not know much about combat, but I know that you synchronise your watches and have a lot of rendezvous. My watch was a lone wolf and I was subject to a non-dezvous.

Or so I thought. I would later learn that the man who was standing with the sign that read 'Patrick Sharpin' was actually there to pick me up. It had crossed my mind at the time but I really thought the armed forces would have done their home-work better than that so gave them the benefit of the doubt and ignored that poor man completely.

It's not a nice feeling to be stranded in a strange land. I was able to track down a taxi and was eventually able to convey to the taxi driver where I wanted to go. I didn't know the name and wasn't sure how much I was allowed to divulge about the camp so just tried to give general descriptions. It was far from easy but, eventually, I got used to his thick accent and we were even able to have a nice chat about his childhood growing up in Sunderland.

For a while, I was a little bit unsure that he had understood where I wanted to go but he was, like a certain charismatic pop hunk, adamant. It was dark by the time I patted my new friend on the shoulder and gave him what I think was a decent tip. It's tough to tell – I'd given him hundreds in the local currency, but he still looked cross.

I took a deep breath and marched with pride towards the camp's gates. Above them was a tattered sign that read 'Mediterranean Club Holiday Resort for 18–30s'. It struck me as a strange name for an army base and I was sure that it wasn't what I'd been told to aim for, but I knew that in war, one must take many things in one's stride.

My only experience of war was through films, so there was no way of knowing that the things that really hit you hard in an actual combat zone are the smells and the sounds. It's hard to describe, but you do feel like you're smelling the essence of humanity. It smelt like electricity and fear and instinct and machismo and mortality with a hint of lemon. I know it's an odd thing to say, but everything was both extremely quiet and extremely loud. There was obviously no form of fighting currently happening but the threat of that, the imminent arrival of potential death, made the still night scream with tension. I could hear my heart beating and crickets chirping as though they were the crescendo of a grand orchestral piece. As the light wind gently weaved its way through the lemon trees, it sounded like a hurricane.

There was little lighting but I was able to find my way to the room in which I'd be staying. The chap behind the desk wasn't very helpful and was extremely scruffy for a member of the armed forces, but he eventually gave me my room key. The door was battered and had a couple of holes, and the paint around it was peeling off. When I stepped inside, I was struck by the starkness of the room. Somebody will have spent their last night in that room and that was a depressing thought. The mucky white wall, battered chair and threadbare mattress meant this was not a fitting preparatory chamber for a martyr's death.

I knew that this wasn't going to be a luxurious venue, but I was still shocked by the environment. This wasn't somewhere to live, this was somewhere to survive. From the stark, barbaric nature of the fencing to the dead plants all around, it was clear that no concession had been made to comfort. It was as if the bleak and unfeeling buildings were specifically designed to harden the soul in readiness to face the darkest aspects of humanity.

I didn't sleep well and kept thinking that I was hearing the sound of bombs. As soon as dawn hit, I could hear my neighbours waking through the thin walls. Thankfully, my early breakfast shows had given me good experience of early starts, so all I needed was a quick yawn and a bit of a stretch and I was ready to go meet the guys.

The loud tranquillity of the night before had been replaced with a more conventional sound and there was plenty of shouting over the background noise of alarms somewhere in the distance. At first, I thought there must be some kind of attack or exercise, but the people around me didn't look unduly worried – or so I thought. All of a sudden, there was a huge rush and I was very nearly pushed clean off the balcony as people rushed past me and flew down the stairs as if their lives depended on it. My heartrate quickened and I followed them, trying to make sense of the shrieks and hollering. The only word that I could make out was 'Germans'.

I didn't know much at all about current affairs. I still don't. For me, the news bulletins were and are a chance to check on the hair and give some thought to which exciting intros and outros I'd do during the next hour's links. I was pretty sure that Argentina was involved in our current war but the revelation that the Germans were also in on it was a worrying development. Dad had always hated the Germans for some malarkey that had occurred when he was a kid but, annoyingly, I'd always been too self-absorbed to ask him exactly what had gone down.

I kept pace with my comrades and was expecting that we would reach some kind of underground bunker. It came as quite a surprise when we arrived at a swimming pool and only then did I see the signs. This was actually a Mediterranean Club Holiday Resort for 18-30s.

'Dammit,' said a pasty fat man to my right, 'I don't know how they manage to get the loungers every single time.'

I sat on the edge of the pool with my legs dangling in from the knee down for about an hour. I received several compliments about my hair from lounger-occupying Germans, which is, of course, the ultimate praise in the mullet world.

I didn't have long to enjoy basking in the glory of that acclaim before an angry general barked at me. I soon realised it was actually the dog by his side that barked and the general then told me in a pleasant tone that my lift had arrived. As I mentioned before, apparently the man at the airport with the sign for 'Patrick Sharpin' had been waiting for me. I obviously ignored him, which led to my hailing a taxi that ultimately took me to the wrong place.

I eventually got to the camp and it was actually pretty nice. The lads I was introduced to were all very friendly and we shared some excellent jokes about the discrepancy between my hairstyle and theirs. I decided to be a bit more serious and talk about their loved ones, sensing that the hardship of being away from our nearest and dearest would provide a good bonding opportunity.

'How long have you been out here?' I asked one guy who had mentioned his wife and son.

'Five months, three days,' he replied.

'That's tough, man. You must miss those guys back home . . .' I said earnestly.

A smile spread across his face as he replied, 'Nah, don't miss 'em a bit!'

A few of the other guys laughed and I felt disgusted. I'm still not sure where it came from, but I launched into a lecture about how much they'd be missing him, how every day they would be sick with worry for his safety. I told him in no uncertain terms that if they meant that little to him, then he needed to let them go because it's not fair for a wife to dote on a husband and a son to look up to his father when he isn't utterly invested in them. I remember there was a pause while the words sunk in, and then he told me he'd been joking and burst into tears. I tried going back to the hair thing to repair the mood but it didn't work.

There was a lot of joking across the camp, which was great to see. I was so impressed that morale could be so high and the guys were all so relaxed, as if their lives were in no danger whatsoever. The studio they had for me to broadcast from was pretty basic but it worked and was pumped into every building in the camp as well as the recreational courtyard.

I should confess that there was quite a lot of booze floating around in the evenings and if anybody is reading this who is from the side of whoever we were fighting over there, you're going to be kicking yourselves that you didn't attack. You'd have caught us with our trousers literally around our ankles on most evenings. The result is that my memory is a bit hazy (not alcohol in my case, mild sunstroke) and that coupled with the fact that the Robin Williams film, *Good Morning, Vietnam*, came out around the same time, means I do blur the boundaries a bit when it comes to memories.

One thing I am pretty sure of, though, is that I wasn't censored. In the film, Robin Williams locks horns with bureaucracy over what he can and can't say on the radio, whereas I was given carte blanche to do and say what I wanted. On one occasion, I played the same Simple Minds song back to back without even a comment, let alone a slap on the wrists. In fact, they left me entirely alone when I was broadcasting and didn't even schedule any debriefing sessions. I was so impressed that even doing what they were doing, they had the time to respect my craft and let it breathe. Also they trusted me and I like to think that I repaid that trust.

I do think back to the Simple Minds débâcle and shudder. I can still see the mistake so clearly. I looked down past my incredibly hairy arms and did one of my trademark voices . . . actually that bit is probably from *Good Morning, Vietnam*. Incidentally, I think the part of that film where the squaddie says he once bumped into Robin's character in a supermarket in Milton Keynes is one of the film's nicest moments. Simple Minds were on the left turntable but, for some reason, I was convinced that I'd put ABC on the left so, at the end of the link, I spun that disc again. I felt better when I later found out that the great John Peel had done the same thing with 'Teenage Kicks' by The Undertones and I do think that the mistake was almost worth it for the cracking link that followed: 'That was Simple Minds there with "Don't You Forget About Me". Well you're not likely to, having heard them back to back just now.' Some people say that if you make a mistake, you shouldn't draw attention to it, but I think it's noble to hold your hands up and, if you can do it with a great line like that one, then you're living the dream.

A lot of the guys told me that the hardest thing was the downtime and it didn't take me long to find that they were right. Second follows second, minute follows minute and hour follows hour. You soon learn that the real war isn't on the battlefield, it's in your head.

I took a collection of First World War poems with me. I don't read that much but, when I do, I tend to like to put myself in the mind of the writer. So, for example, I read *High Fidelity* at the back of HMV by the posters; *1984* in 1984; and I read *Far from the Madding Crowd* as far away from a madding crowd as I could get. I thought that reading those war poems in the middle of a war would add something to them and, boy, was I right.

Naturally, I was drawn to Siegfried Sassoon. The humid air was wreaking havoc with my hair and I was desperate to see what Vidal's dad (it has to be right?) could tell me about the situation. It was a bit disappointing, to be honest, and I didn't really take anything from those poems. There was one line that stuck with me: 'December stillness, teach me through your trees . . . That loom along the west, one with the land . . . The veiled evangel of your mysteries . . .' I think that's to do with split ends but I'm not entirely sure. Still, lack of practical hair tips aside, there's some all right stuff in those poems. I thought the bit about using trees as an educational tool was good. You can learn a lot from nature – have you ever seen a capybara with dandruff? Some of the poetry had a profound effect on me and I'd sometimes ponder the fleeting nature of all things and the mysteries of the universe while, using little more than muscle memory, I back-announced Kajagoogoo.

I can see why so many of those guys back in the First World War turned to poetry. With all that time inside your own head and faced by the prospect of your own mortality, you definitely reach new levels of profundity and emotion. I think it's a bit like how diamonds get formed. You have this tremendous pressure bearing down on something for what seems like an eternity and, at the end, something beautiful is born.

I didn't have myself down as a poetry guy, I really didn't, but after a while it felt like something I wanted to do. A bit more time passed and then it became something that I was compelled to do. By the end of that second day, I reached for a pen and paper. The thing I found about writing war poetry is that it's very hard to look back over what you've written and not find that you've written the lyrics to 'War' by Edwin Starr.

After the twelfth time that happened, I decided to go for a different approach. Instead of focussing on the war aspect, I thought I'd think about missing my darling other half. I still have the poem and, although it may be a bit mushy in places, I want to include it here. I never could think of a title:

I miss you like the deserts miss the cooling rain
I miss you like I did the 11:27 train
I miss you like US colour misses the letter u
I miss you like Black Lace miss the success of 'Agadoo'
I miss you like the woods can make us miss the trees
I miss you like romantics miss proper hotel keys
I miss you like albinos miss having melanin
I miss you like the houses that the homeless miss dwelling in
I miss you like flour spelled this way misses having pretty petals
I miss you like mercury misses having-a-state-of-matter-at-room-
*   temperature-in-common-with-other-metals*
I miss you like the grass at noon misses glist'ning dew
I miss you like Bowie's left eye misses being blue
I miss you like the lonely miss getting letters in the post
I miss you like over-sleepers miss having morning toast
I miss you like a widow will miss her beloved spouse
I miss you like the homeless still miss living in that house
Still, I'm back tomorrow so that will be nice.

I read the poem out to the guys who all gave me plenty of constructive feedback. I didn't use any of it, though, because I thought that would cheapen the message and personal element. I'm happy to say the poem was gratefully received, although the fact that I got home nearly a full week before it arrived was a bit of a shame. My second offering, about the man from Nantucket, was more popular.

I couldn't quite believe it when my time to leave the camp came. The main emotion I experienced was one of guilt. I was getting to go home, whereas the other guys were still going to be stuck out there doing their thing. I'd given them the gift of music and elite-level presenting but it didn't feel like enough. I spent my last morning trying to think of something I could do. What was it that I could give them or do for them? How could I show my affection for them as men and admiration for them as soldiers? In the end, I couldn't think of anything so left it but I think the length and strength of my hugs encapsulated some of what I wanted to say. Also, on the plane I realised that I'd left my toothpaste behind so I'm sure that somebody appreciated that. I took a last look around the camp after finishing my final broadcast. It seemed so much smaller now that I knew I was leaving.

The one thing that I'd maintained all along was that I didn't want a fuss when I left. I got my wish. I had been to war but now I had to return to my homeland and deal with the small matter of the rest of my life. And a certain fun house (*Fun House*).

Chapter 8

ABBA – 'Dancing Queen'

Probably the second best song written about dancing after Pat and Mick's 'I Haven't Stopped Dancing Yet'. The very slow trickle of royalties that still comes in is a reminder that some people somewhere still haven't stopped and that always fills my heart.

I've always made sure I'm up on the charts, not because I'm an especially big fan of music but because it provides opportunities for material between songs on air and at dinner parties off it. I remember saying to Anthea Turner at one particular soirée that the only thing worse than 'Sex on Fire' was 'Come on Eileen'. Ouch, if looks could kill. I never imagined for one minute I would end up part of radio's between-banter songs but God, like U2, moves in mysterious ways. That's another one of mine and one that Fred Dineage was charitable enough to say 'almost works'.

While my experiences serving my country were not something I would wish to repeat any time soon, psychologically they were an essential part of my development. That's something a lot of people forgot when they raucously celebrated Maggie Thatcher's death with street parties – it was the making of at least one fledgling DJ.

After the horrors I had seen, I knew I had to do something

great with my time on this earth. Life is a fleeting, fragile thing. One minute you're Vanilla Ice in 1990, the next you're Vanilla Ice in 1995. If the brutal reality of modern warfare had taught me anything, it was that I did not want to become known for one breakthrough hip-hop single and end up a punchline.

As the 1980s wore on, I entered a dark phase. The things which had always brought me joy suddenly did nothing for me. Perhaps it was what I'd seen during the war or maybe it was a darkness within me. I was in a funk and not the cool '70s James Brown kind. It was as though I had a stone in my shoe perpetually, a stone that could not be removed no matter how much Duran Duran I listened to. Incidentally, I have long advocated synthpop as a means of tackling depression – I even wrote a letter to then Secretary of State for Health Kenneth Clarke suggesting that the NHS take this into consideration, but the reply was a 'no'. Was it the ultrasound treatment that cured my neighbour Nigel's kidney stones, or was it my Ultravox mixtape? We can never know, but I have my suspicions.

When the Atari no longer brings you happiness and you're sick to death of the Rubik's Cube, what is a man to do? It is a question that has baffled humans for millennia and it was one I felt entirely unable to answer. Fortunately, it is always darkest just before the dawn and salvation, in the form of pop music (isn't it always?) was just around the corner.

In life, we are all basically babies and when we're unhappy we're usually after a change. I thought all I wanted was to be on the radio until my dying day, but what I hadn't realised is that the radio doesn't solely involve disc jockeys. There are also the song jockeys, too – those people more commonly referred to as musicians.

It was a crisp autumn day when the call came through, the kind of day where anything seems possible and the mullet has just the right amount of bounce. For the first time in a long time, things just felt right.

The man on the other end of the line introduced himself, although he needed no introduction for a man as well versed in pop music as I was.

'Hey, Pat, this is Mike Stock of Stock Aitken Waterman fame. The lads say hi.'

There was the distant sound of pleasantries. This was before the era of conference calls and I'm fairly sure they all lived together to make things easier. Mike shushed his colleagues then uttered the immortal words: 'Do you mind coming into the office for a meeting at some point? We've had a brainwave and we think you might be just the man we're after.'

Did I mind having a meeting with one of the most successful songwriting and producing partnerships of all time? Yes, I did . . . not! (*Wayne's World* came out a few years later and I would become fairly obsessed with the 'not' joke format and it's something I'm unable to shake to this day, much to my wife's chagrin.)

A few days later and I was sitting in the plush offices of SAW (yet another one of my inventive abbreviations) sipping a Dr Pepper and listening to the pitch while wondering, naturally, what was the worst that could happen. I've often seen myself as one of life's Dr Peppers – so misunderstood but fundamentally good. Others say we're alike in that we're both rubbish but potato, potato (a phrase that works better aloud). It transpired that the three guys had happened upon one of the greatest musical duos in the history of popular music. In Pete Waterman's words, 'Imagine a cross between Simon and Garfunkel and Hall and Oates and Pet Shop and Boys.'

This double act apparently had it all. There was just one stumbling block – the name. Stock, Aitken and Waterman always came up with the name first and everything else followed.

This time they had come up with the perfect name for a vocal duo and that name was Pat and Mick. The brilliant act they'd discovered happened to be called Matt and Rick but a miss is as good as a mile. They were great dancers, incredible singers and oozed charisma from every orifice but they had come last in the lottery of life when it came to what they'd been christened (figuratively speaking that is – I'm fairly sure Rick was Jewish).

I was at Capital FM by this point and a fellow DJ named Mick was roped in to partner me. The initial idea was that the record label would buy Matt and Rick's stuff for us to perform and they would have a decent career as songwriters. Unfortunately, because he didn't really understand the industry, Matt was adamant that he wouldn't sell, something about how 'a name is just a name, this is a fucking disgrace'. Typical diva! He kept banging on about roses smelling like roses no matter what they're called and I said that an arse smells like an arse no matter what it's called and Matt accepted defeat.

Since we had already committed to something of a golden handcuffs deal, the label were stuck with us (their words). And as we couldn't write music and Matt was refusing to budge, Aitken came up with the most innovative and original solution imaginable – we would record cover versions. We decided together that all the proceeds should go to Capital's Help a London Child charity appeal and that was a joint decision that we were definitely all delighted about.

With the dream team assembled, the next key question was what we were going to cover. I was listening to a lot of Tchaikovsky at the time and Aitken was obsessive about early Bach ('before he sold out' – his words). 'Nessun Dorma' was a piece we really felt we could bring something to and it was especially irritating when Pavarotti received such acclaim for it a couple of years later at the 1990 World Cup.

We walked into our first big meeting with the label adamant that we would do something with a classical feel and lyrical complexity. We left that meeting in absolute agreement that we'd cover a bunch of disco hits. This business is about nothing if it's not about compromise.

Our first single was a cover of 'Let's All Chant' by the Michael Zager Band, a late '70s disco belter that we lent a late '80s twist. Astonishingly, it was released under the name Mick and Pat. This made literally no sense; if we were going to have a name as rubbish as that then they might as well have just let Rick and Matt release it. The higher-ups fobbed me off with some nonsense about alphabetical order being important but I, like the Great British public by the end of our musical career, wasn't buying it. The remainder of our singles would be rightly released under the Pat and Mick name and, after hours spent lobbying on my behalf, it's in that order when you go on to our Wikipedia page.

The video, available on YouTube, is a kind of masterpiece. There are 1,320 thumbs up and 48 thumbs down on that video at the time of writing and that tells its own story. I could, however, live without Bob Blob's contribution in the comments section underneath: 'Here's a good drinking game for you. Take a shot after every time you think these guys are acting gay. See how f★★★ed you are by the end of the song!'

Our second single, a cover of Gonzalez's 'Haven't Stopped Dancing Yet', entered the charts in the Top 10 and we were absolutely elated. The naysayers might claim it only got that high because all proceeds were going to charity but I just don't buy it. We had something more tangible than the basic human need to give money to homeless children in our nation's capital. We had the X factor before the *X Factor* was even a thing – I like to think of it as the W Factor. My one regret was that no interviewer ever asked me how I felt about the song's success. I spent hours practising my knowing wink while announcing, 'I haven't stopped dancing yet!' Sometimes life is cruel.

When it was time to make the video for 'Haven't Stopped Dancing Yet', we had some amazing ideas. A friend of a friend knew Terrence Malick and there was talk that the film genius might just come out of his self-imposed exile to work with us. We wanted something avant-garde and provocative, a minia-ture film that would capture the existential turmoil of human beings literally unable to stop dancing. The label disagreed and so it was another video largely comprised of us dancing on stage at a club flanked by attractive women. You can't have every-thing. Or, as we felt at the time, you can't have anything.

The most exciting thing for any new artist during that era was the chance to be on *TOTP*. The lights, the cameras, the backstage vol-au-vents. We couldn't believe we would finally get to go on national television and hobnob backstage with celebrities galore. A true once in a lifetime opportunity to do something generations of young people had always fantasised about doing. This was somewhat punctured by my wife pointing out that, because of my presenting duties, I'd been on a bunch of times already.

The thing is, being a featured act is quite different to hosting. It's like the difference between being a guest at a party and hosting. There is so little responsibility involved in just turning up, making small-talk (singing), having some pitta and hummus (dancing) then going home (leaving the stage). As a host, however, be it of a small gathering at home or a television institution beamed into living rooms up and down the country, you are the facilitator of dreams.

I struggled to make this adjustment. On our first *TOTP* appearance as musical guests, I was unable to help myself. When I heard the familiar refrain of '5, 4, 3 . . .' and the camera panned round, I acted on instinct.

'Here's Big Country's new single, "In a Big Country"!'

Time and again I would introduce the next act. I couldn't help myself, it's just who I am. Presenting is in my blood. On the eighth take, I finally remembered to sing the song but if you look carefully at the footage you can see that there's something very wrong behind the eyes.

We released eight singles between 1988 and 1993, culminating with 'Hot Hot Hot', a Top 47 smash that entered the charts at 47. We made a lot of money for charity but eventually even the philanthropic aspect was dwarfed by my increasing bitterness. We were still being employed as presenters on a semi-regular basis and I just couldn't keep the hostility out of my voice when announcing the Top 20 if we weren't in it.

I suppose the double act is considered a bit of a joke now,

something that was really hammered home when we were asked to appear on the Identity Parade round on *Never Mind the Buzzcocks* back in 2010. Still, £65 is £65 and you can't eat your principles. Plus, many people have said to me that we came out of the whole thing with a lot of dignity and they weren't all family members.

People can laugh all they want but I like to think we paved the way for a generation of artists who transitioned from TV to music. Without us, there probably wouldn't be a Will Smith and there certainly wouldn't be an Ant and Dec. The key difference between us and the latter is that people could actually tell us apart. Does that make us a superior partnership? That's not for me to say. But yes.

Hunter S Thompson summed things up best I think: 'The music business is a cruel and shallow money trench, a long plastic hallway where thieves and pimps run free, and good men die like dogs. There's also a negative side.'

What I needed now was a project that would be wacky, fun and outrageous. And I thought I had a good idea for just what that might be.

Chapter 9

Puccini – 'Nessun Dorma'

This song never fails to bring a tear to my eyes, and crave a Cornetto – even though it's a different song. Probably the finest World Cup anthem ever to be written by a mushroom.

When you're a pop star on *TOTP*, it's easy to think that you've peaked. I remember one of our backing dancers squeezing my hand just before what was to be our final appearance and saying, 'This is so cool! Even if I don't achieve anything else, I've done this. I'll always have this.' It's just as well he felt that way. *TOTP* is the zenith for many people – Pato Banton, Babylon Zoo, that dancer; but it's also a stepping stone on the way up for others – Ant and Dec, Mark Wahlberg, me. Somehow, I knew that something else was in store for old Patmandu.

People almost never describe me as 'not just a pretty face' which I can only assume is a testament to the fact that my multi-faceted skill set is widely accepted. I like having ideas and to this day wonder if I'm constantly firing the synapses in my brain because of my life in radio, or if I found my life in radio because of my relentless synapse action. Some of the ideas were small, such as laughing while back-announcing a song even though nothing funny had happened or putting my feet on the desk for a promotional photo. But one of my ideas was big; it was so much more than the split-second diffusion of a neurotransmitter across a junction between two nerve cells. It was a slow process, percolating like a rich Java, fermenting like a rich wine, stewing like a rich stew.

I hadn't really been aware it was there until it suddenly showed itself to me in a phone call with my agent. As soon as I picked up the phone, I knew what he was going to say. 'Hello,' he said. He went on to say that some television executives had been in touch and they were looking to get some new faces into children's television. That was the moment that the idea announced itself to me. It was perfectly formed and, like the coffee, wine and stew referenced in the similes above, ready to drink/drink/eat.

'Set up a meeting,' I told my agent and hung up.

He called back moments later. 'We already have . . . we're doing a breakfast tomorrow at 9.30am.'

'Perfect. They're in for a treat,' I replied and hung up again.

He phoned again instantaneously. 'Is this line OK? We keep getting cut off.'

'The line, like the idea I have, is flawless. Tomorrow will be a breakfast of champions,' I announced before triumphantly hanging up for what I mistakenly thought was the last time.

'Just thought you might want to know where the breakfast is,' intoned my agent upon my answering for a fourth time in fifteen seconds.

The breakfast was divine. Tea, toast and a poached egg. 'If a poached rhino tastes half as good as this, I can see why all those guys in Africa are willing to break the law,' I said with a beaming smile to our waitress. She blushed and I felt the rest of the table crawl into the palm of my hand. We had already discussed the desire of Scottish Television Productions (part of the STV Group) to create a game show for kids but not what the show would be. ITV were apparently interested and were waiting for a pitch. I don't remember exactly how many ideas the producers gave me but it was about four or five. One was to be a live-action version of snakes and ladders although that was quickly dispelled on health and safety grounds. The splinter risk was simply too great. Another was a quiz that was based around the life and times of mathematician Pierre de Fermat but that was shelved almost immediately because a rival company had something very similar in production. I am proud to say that there was one round on *Fun House* where the kids had to retrieve the numbers and letters of a simple equation from inside a giant trifle. I called it 'The Proof Is in the Pudding' as a tribute to Fermat. That rival idea changed quite a lot over the course of its production and you'll know it now as *The Really Wild Show*.

Following my explanation of *Fun House*, there was a stunned silence. I can't remember exactly what happened next because the mind always plays tricks when it comes to key moments in one's life but I can say for certain that the producers all carried me out of the room on their shoulders. My agent informs me that we had some celebratory drinks and I overdid it in a frankly unacceptable way. Ribena has always had a strange effect on me; I think it's the E numbers.

The next morning I had a bit of a sore head but I can tell you the best hangover cure is two aspirin and a production meeting for a new gameshow. We had a tremendous team in to brainstorm although I had a very strong sense of what the show should be. It's hard to describe but everything was crystal clear in my mind. Years later, I would recall my trip to Florida and how I saw the show on American television and had lifted the idea wholesale but I don't think that in any way detracts from anything.

Everyone got on board with the idea very quickly and I could feel my vision taking shape. I can't take full credit though, there was an amazing team and a lot of what you see in those beautiful, beautiful episodes is thanks to the work of the many great minds that I was lucky enough to work with. There were a couple of stumbling blocks early on but that's the nature of the game. The first of these was our plan to use gunk. The show had to be messy. Kids love chaos and what's more joyous than running around, knocking stuff over and making a right old mess. We wanted something to be right at the heart of that mess. Could it be paper? We thought about having reams and reams of paper about the place but that was a rubbish idea. Somebody suggested that it should be a liquid so we experimented with water (too boring), milk (still too boring), mild acids (problematic), champagne (expensive) and countless others before somebody else said it should be somewhere between a liquid and a solid. 'You mean like a slime?' I asked and that person said, 'Yes, like a slime.'

It didn't take long before we had developed a prototype gunk. It was gloopy and colourful and only mildly toxic but something about it didn't sit right with me. It was after our second broadcast that the lawyers came in. They represented an American show accusing us of spying, corruption and blackmail to get our hands on their gunk recipe and dismissed out of hand the notion that we had come up with the same recipe independently. Considering that recipe was flour, water and food colouring, we probably had a decent case but a team of American lawyers is quite intimidating so we settled out of court.

The result was that we came up with a completely new recipe that had a little bit more flour in it and we gave it a different name – 'gunge'. It was one of the most rewarding moments of my life. That nagging feeling that something wasn't right with the gunk was gone and replaced with a calmness, a oneness. They say that when you're in love, the arts take on a new meaning and their full beauty finally presents itself to you. That may be a classical painting or it may be the cover of 'It's in His Kiss' by Cher. I can't tell you exactly what changed in that wondrous moment when I pushed a young runner's head into a bucket of gunge, but what I can tell you is that the next time I went to the National Portrait Gallery and the next time I tuned into Magic FM, I had tears in my eyes. Plenty of DJs consider listening to other stations something of a busman's holiday, but I've never lost that childlike glee about the medium. I'm just lucky I suppose.

Another little bump was when my mate, Dave, found out about the project and asked to be involved. Dave had had some real success as the bloke who played Bungle on *Rainbow* but he really wanted to get his face out there and branch out with some work that didn't see him trapped inside a giant bear suit. I'm nothing if not a loyal friend and assured Dave there was room for him by my side. I would, after all, need a sidekick.

It was unfortunate that they had already decided on the cheerleader costume as it was not terribly flattering on poor Dave (although nobody can deny that the man knows his way around a pom-pom). It was also unfortunate that a pair of talented twins had been found and that, coincidentally, the costumes were a perfect fit. Dave very nearly backed out of the audition but I told him I had faith in him (which I absolutely did). We recorded two pilots, one with him and one with the twins. He absolutely nailed it. Sure, the costume looked weird and didn't fit him at all, but Dave bonded with the contestants and injected a wonderful energy into the show. I was gobsmacked when we took a vote and I was the only person backing him. How could I be the only one to see that he was perfect? It was like the emperor's new clothes, and not just because Dave's cock and balls were quite clearly on display.

Ultimately, it was Dave's insistence on being a single entity that was his downfall. As the executive producer said to me, there are two teams and two twins but only one Dave. There is indeed only one Dave and I still love you, buddy.

I've spoken to the twins about my vote and I'm happy to say that it has been the cause of absolutely no friction between us. The scurrilous rumours about us having a threesome, however, have made things a bit strained at times and I apologise unreservedly for starting them. As you'll read later, those university gigs can bring out the worst in you.

Ideas flew around the room so thick and fast that we took to recording the meetings. I still have a number of the tapes lying around and on rainy days I'll sometimes listen back for old times' sake. It's funny how the memory works. I feel like I can recall those meetings verbatim and yet it was actually quite different. Here's a snippet I've transcribed to give you a sense of what it was like:

Pat: . . . I just think I'd rather be dead than have that many split ends.

Bob: OK, guys. Canteen says they're out of coffee.

Pat: That's all right . . . just give me a cup of that horrible hot brown stuff they normally serve!

(Laughter, but less than I remember)

Bob: So we're thinking about the set today . . .

Pat: I've drawn up some designs and have some colour schemes here . . . I'll just talk you through. It's a minimalist design and as you can see the font has very clean edges which matches the flanks of the set. Colour-wise I've gone for a very tasteful monochrome that moves from black to a deep charcoal. It's timeless and elegant . . .

Bob: Sorry, Pat, I'm not sure we're on the same page.

Pat: Were you thinking something a bit more neoclassical?

Bob: I was thinking more colour. Like really in your face, migraine-inducing colour.

Pat: Oh, so like maybe add some light peach to the trim?

Bob: I was thinking like all of the colours. Look at your jumper.

Sian: Right. So more like one of Boy George's hats has eaten a box of Crayola and thrown it all up.

Bob: Exactly. OK, so the theme music . . .

Pat: I thought we agreed on 'Nessun Dorma'?

Sian: The rights are proving difficult to get.

Pat: Well, I'm happy to throw as much money as we need at it.

Bob: Yes, you've been quite clear about that.

Pat: I bloody love 'Nessun Dorma'.

Bob: Yes, you've expressed your feelings many times.

Pat: It means 'none shall sleep'.

Bob: Yes, you've mentioned. Now just as a contingency, I have had somebody knock up a tune for us.

Pat: What sort of thing? String arrangement or something more choral?

Bob: It's just a catchy tune that we'll chuck some banal lyrics over. Now, we discussed some kind of list of adjectives as a catchphrase. Pat, you said you'd knock something together.

Pat: Sure did. I've got it here. So I was thinking we have different voices that shout out, 'It's wacky, it's fun, it's crazy, it's maudlin, it's capricious, it's stimulating, it's outrageous!' And then you get the opening strains of 'Nessun Dorma'.

Bob: Sure. I think it starts well and ends well but loses its way slightly. Did you say 'maudlin'?

Pat: Yeah, I thought it would be good to get some texture in there. Add some depth to the character of the house.

Sian: The house is fun. That's all it needs to be.

Pat: But often if you scratch just below the surface, there's a complexity, a darkness. You know, it's like the sad clown thing. A lot of the liveliest, funniest people are actually cripplingly sad.

Bob: It's just a fun house, Pat.

Pat: We can talk it through.

It was some weeks before we got on to discussing what the games would be. For some reason, that was quite difficult and we sat in silence for hours waiting for inspiration to strike. Finally, something came to me and I leapt to my feet. 'Apple-bobbing!' I announced with my finger pointing to the heavens. We bobbed for apples for roughly two hours and when we came back we were all in a much better headspace to think of games. The key was deciding that the kids should have to collect things but in a way that meant they would keep falling over. If you've seen the show, you'll know that this simple format can be repeated in an endless variety of ways that keeps it fresh and exciting.

We all agreed that we wanted to be able to test the kids' mental agility as well as the physical. One of the producers suggested some kind of mock interrogation where points would be awarded for how long they could go without cracking. The general consensus was that it would slow the pace of the show and take too long to reach the breaking point of contestants. It might sound silly but the creator of *Mastermind* was genuinely inspired to create the show by his experiences being interrogated by the Gestapo during the Second World War. I suggested only broadcasting the final couple of minutes of the process but it was rightly pointed out that to enjoy the dénouement of a good interrogation you need to have seen the whole thing to allow the tension to build properly and provide the satisfying pay-off. It's very similar to the way highlights will never do justice to a Test match, whatever Dave Benson Phillips might tell you.

Instead, it was agreed that there would be a trivia question at the end of each round. These questions were normally pretty easy and I'm often asked why they were worth the same amount of points as the physical ordeal of the game that preceded them. I'd like to say it was a comment on how society in the late '80s and early '90s valued knowledge over hard work but, in truth, it was just sloppiness when it came to internal consistency.

In our first non-broadcast pilot, we went straight from the games into the Fun House but it all felt a bit rushed. The production all agreed that something was missing. Bob went on holiday to Florida and, when he came back, he did so with the final piece of the jigsaw. 'Go-karts,' he said and, after we all spent two hours go-karting, we thought we could actually just put a go-kart race in the show, which I think worked pretty well.

As I've said, I have a lot of time for the twins (in fact, these days, I have a lot of time for anybody who happens to be available) and one of the many wonderful things they brought to the show was counting. This is the sort of thing that separates the good from the great in the world of gameshow assistants. When counting tokens or balloons or little discs, most people would say 'One, two, three, four . . .' (assuming they needed to get to four). What the twins did was really raise the inflection of the last number so that it was almost more of a cheer than a word. They'd count by saying, 'One, two, three, *four!*' What I also loved about their approach was how they would do the same thing regardless of how many items the contestants had gathered. Thirteen would be said as '. . . *thirteen!*' and two would be delivered as '. . . *two!*' Even though two is a terrible score and those kids should have been deeply embarrassed, they were made to feel as if they weren't useless and I think that's a nice thing.

You probably remember that, whenever the show started, I would come out and deliver some great gag. It would be the first thing I said and set the perfect tone for the ensuing fun. The maxim 'always open with a joke' has always served me well and it wouldn't surprise me to learn that the opening joke was the favourite part of the show for some people who I'm sure will let me know sooner or later. What a lot of people don't realise is that it was my idea. In fact, not only was it my idea, but I absolutely insisted on it and the producers actually tried to talk me out of it. If you look on YouTube, you can see the start of an episode where I'm on a bike and I say, 'So, this is what the boss meant when he said, "On your bike!"' It's a bit of a shame that each time the editors cut straight into music or something, which eats into where the laugh would be, but in a show so short you really do need to be super-efficient to get everything in.

Jokes, cars, gunge and twins were the secrets of our success. And fun. Now we just had to make the pilot and see whether the people responded.

Chapter 10

Fun House – Theme Tune

For obvious reasons (royalties).

They say you never forget your first time . . . and they're not wrong. After countless hours sitting in stuffy production meetings spitballing ideas, blowing bubbles with gum and losing pencils in my hair, it was finally time to make the pilot. I've often wondered about the word 'pilot', seeing as it can mean both 'trying something out' and 'having the responsibility of safely transporting persons inside a giant, complicated metal tube thousands of feet in the air'. Let's hope never the twain shall meet. Unless it's some kind of reality vehicle, in which case sign me up.

Occasionally, life offers you the perfect metaphor. Those with a long memory (or Challenge TV, either works) will recall that my first appearance on *Fun House,* like so many others, involved me entering the set on a go-kart. Whether the director made this decision deliberately because he knew this was the first time I'd had my own 'vehicle', or whether it was just to foreshadow the go-kart race later in the show, we may never know. In a way, it doesn't really matter.

So much goes into making a television programme, but I don't think Joe Public has ever really appreciated that. It may have looked like unrestrained mayhem but there was a military precision to how we pitted these two sets of gladiators head to head in a modern-day Colosseum utilising all the athletic prowess and intellectual savvy they could muster. My favourite bits were always when the kids got all messy.

It seems like only yesterday that we shot that first episode but that might just be because I watched it again last night in preparation for writing this chapter. Incidentally, that's one in the eye for my wife who suggested we chuck out the VHS player years ago. You can't put a price on memories (although a VCR goes for about £100 on eBay these days).

After I'd got off the go-kart, it was time to deliver my first joke. The key with television is to make sure you're communicating mainly with the audience at home but without those in the studio feeling like they're being short-changed.

'Now here's the guy who puts the *fun* into *Fun House* . . . Pat Sharp!'

Those were the words of the announcer that were ringing in my ears as I dismounted the vehicle and prepared myself for the moment I'd acted out in front of the mirror since I was old enough to dream and stand, and correctly use a mirror. So much pressure. If I was the man who put the fun into *Fun House* then, without me, this was nothing more than a house. A humdrum, boring, run-of-the-mill abode. I cleared my throat, instinctively ran my fingers through my hair and, after several minutes of ecstatic follicle-based bliss, remembered where I was and said: 'What did the mushroom say to the fungus? You're a fun guy (fungi)!'

They say you can only truly relax once you've got your first laugh. All that pent-up anxiety and tension is released when the

On the set of *Fun House* in happier
times *(from left to right)* Martina/
Melanie, me, Melanie/Martina.
(© STV)

Moments after imparting my sizeable wisdom to Lady Di.
(© Princess Diana Archive/Stringer/Getty Images)

It was only at the very end of
this nightclub opening that I
realised these weren't the twins.
(© Raymond Field/Shutterstock)

You can see the pain in my face as Gemma Collins's golden locks remind me of all I'd lost. (© *Ken McKay/ITV/ Shutterstock*)

(from left to right) Me, Martina/Melanie, Melanie/Martina.
(© *Ken McKay/ITV/ Shutterstock*)

With the Capital FM gang. It took seven takes to get a shot without the mullet dangling into my champagne glass.
(© *Shutterstock*)

Old habits die hard – here I'm desperate to release the barnet from the cruel confines of an oppressive hat. *(© ITV/Shutterstock)*

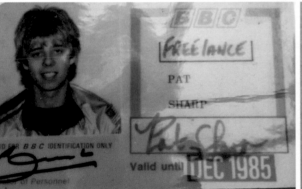

Much like me, this pass worked until the end of 1985.

Being on a stamp is a huge honour. In the past 60 years it's literally just been me, the Queen and over 750 different series of between 1 and 30 images.

Sometimes I put this on and pretend it's still 1989. The rest of the time I don't wear the mask.

With Bros after I introduced them at the O2. *(from left to right)* Luke/Matt, me, Matt/Luke.

The King and I.

You spend twenty minutes securing the perfect selfie only to get photobombed by Tony Hadley when you nail it.

After four months of research, brainstorming and focus groups, along with hundreds of thousands of pounds in consultancy fees, we finally came up with the perfect band name: Pat and Mick.
(Tim Roney/Getty Images)

THIS IS YOUR JUNGLE LIFE

For years I referred to this as 'The Jungle Book'. I was touched by how many people thought it was utterly brilliant and were stunned I had the original copy.

With Michael McIntyre. We went to the same educational institution – the school of hard knocks. (And Merchant Taylors' in Northwood).

Chris Moyles is a great DJ but terrible at framing photos of somebody doing a really good impression of the emperor in *Gladiator.*

With Rita Ora. I kept calling her 'Kia' but I don't think she was amused.

With Jason Donovan and his amazing technicolor white T-shirt.

With Christmas* Tarrant.

*Chris

I'd wanted to meet David Seaman for years before this picture was taken but the power of my hair and his 'tache meant it was too dangerous to be in the same room.

Moments after reminding the Hoff about our time together on the falling Berlin Wall. His memory was as blurry as this photo.

I thought I'd really made a statement with this waistcoat only to be upstaged by one of the other guests opting for a bow tie.

With Andrew Ridgeley. From leather to tweed, tropical clubs to award-winning pubs and George to me.

In my element DJing to a festival of thousands while a cameraman gets some great footage of my money maker.

audience is certain they are in safe hands and can trust the performer without reservation. It really was a godsend when I finally got that first laugh in the middle of Series 6.

To be fair, the director and floor manager had warned me that the fungi gag might be a bit complex for an audience comprised exclusively of pre-teens, especially without the brackets I've been able to employ above; but I always felt my role was to educate as well as entertain. If one kid went home and asked their parents to explain a laboured pun, I felt I'd had a good show. The production team disagreed in the most violent terms imaginable.

Part of the reason the gags so often fell flat has remained a secret until now. This is the kind of juicy showbiz gossip that autobiographies are all about and I have no doubt that the tabloids will be clamouring to serialise this section. I can exclusively reveal that we filmed the show in front of a tiny audience. No doubt when you watched the show at the time or even on Sky or YouTube since, you've seen a packed house of excitable children. Well, I'm not even a natural blond, so appearances can be deceiving . . .

People have sporadically asked me over the years why we filmed the show in Scotland when the bulk of the 'talent' (their inverted commas) hailed from London. There was a very simple reason for this and it was a little something I like to refer to as child labour law loopholes. We were up against the clock in terms of the production timeline and sometimes had to film as many as three or four episodes in a single day. We rightly realised it wasn't fair to keep upwards of a hundred kids stuck in a studio until three in the morning but reckoned it was probably all right if we limited it to just seven youngsters. Scotland is a remarkably progressive place with regard to child labour and the youth up there are allowed to work for far longer. This, for obvious reasons, is ideal.

But how was it we were able to fool all of the people all of the time and convince them that the crowd was actually huge even if my sophisticated wordplay sounded like it landed in an empty room? Simple, really – skilful editing and masterful establishing shots. My work on *Fun House* has absolutely convinced me that Stanley Kubrick faked the moon landings and it has been the cause of untold arguments with Margaret from *The Apprentice*. And if you think she's cutting on telly, you cannot begin to imagine what she's like when there aren't cameras around – the woman's language would put a sailor to shame.

My least favourite part of the show came next as I introduced the teams, a sequence invariably preceded by Martina and Melanie jumping up and down on the spot in their entirely imitable way. In life, there are no rehearsals but, on television, there really should be. Still, time was of the essence, so we made do.

I was always given one scrap of information about each team member and I insisted I free-form my way around the topic like some kind of jazz maestro. It's all well and good when you're dealing with talented performers like those on *Whose Line Is It Anyway?* as they're aware that a participant should accept what another participant has stated and then expand on that line of thinking to keep things going, but it sometimes seemed like a lot of these children didn't even have a basic grounding in improv.

If you watch that first episode, you'll see what a thankless task it was. Ryan on the yellow team had informed a researcher he was a big fan of weightlifting and the exchange on air went as follows:

Pat: Ryan, you're into weightlifting . . .

Ryan: Sometimes.

Pat: Sometimes? OK. It says here you like Arnold Schwarzenegger and you would like to be a future Mr Universe possibly . . .

Ryan: Yeah.

(Pause, seemingly endless)

Pat: (indicating flexing muscles) Give us the old . . . give us the old arms, let's see what you've got up there.

(Thankfully, Ryan does as he's told)

Pat: (Sarcastically) That's fantastic, tremendous. I should think you're almost there, Ryan.

(An outstanding roll of the eyes from Pat that would become a hall-mark of Ricky Gervais and Stephen Merchant's The Office *many years later and for which the presenter would receive not a penny in royalties.)*

As should be obvious, that is patently bad television. Yes, I managed to elevate it in places but the point stands that it reads like some kind of avant-garde experimental theatre piece and even my natural wit and *joie de vivre* can't completely salvage it. People wanted a fun house and not some Pinteresque nonsense that made everyone uncomfortable. That's the problem with no rehearsals, though. Fail to prepare, prepare to fail.

Tommy Cooper died on stage at Her Majesty's Theatre during a live TV recording and the crowd simply assumed it was a gag and laughed uproariously. I died during just about every show we did but, annoyingly, couldn't elicit the same kind of response.

The strange thing about telly is that you can have all the meetings in the world but sometimes magic happens in a way that nobody could have prepared for and it's better than anything you could possibly have written (the fungi joke aside). One key moment during the pilot was when Tony from the red team slipped and fell during a challenge involving copious amounts of gunge and water balloons. The floor was bound to get slippery but somehow none of us had foreseen such a calamity. The silence was uncanny, the kind usually reserved for one of my jokes. We cut to an advert break while Martina, Melanie and I pondered new careers. Then something peculiar happened that was quite unlike anything we'd experienced on the show up until that point – the audience started laughing. Gently at first, but it gradually built to a glorious crescendo of hysteria and joy. Seconds before, our hearts had been in our mouths, but now we realised what great television it was and kids falling over became a central feature of the show. Oh, and it's probably worth noting that *You've Been Framed* began airing on ITV in April the following year. I still watch with a smile on my face knowing that the joy, and prizes of £250, are probably almost entirely my doing.

There were teething problems but that's simply the nature of any creative endeavour. Mystic Meg once reliably informed me that the first draft of *Moby Dick* didn't even involve a whale and it's important that people realise the perfect version of something isn't achieved overnight. Case in point was the thorny issue of the gunge. As outlined in the previous chapter, we knew early on that gunge would be essential if *Fun House* was going to be a success. Unfortunately, the original manufacturers (who I won't name as they don't deserve the oxygen of publicity) made a catastrophic error.

Before the first episode aired on TV, we filmed a little something called a non-broadcast pilot. It's a pretty standard industry thing where you record the show as a trial run and the big dogs get to decide whether you're on to a winner. I knew this was all just a formality because our show was far too good to fail, but sometimes you have to jump through hoops (something that would become a literal part of the show in later years).

That episode, which has never been aired and is the stuff of legend in industry circles, was not without its hiccups. The first issue was Dave, who'd taken the news about the twins pretty badly. His heckling was a major distraction and he was eventually ejected by security in a blur of blood, vomit and promises of vengeance. Apparently, he had been struggling with some self-esteem issues but eventually found salvation through ICA (Identity Crisis Anonymous) and, at the behest of my wife, I begrudgingly accepted his apology once he reached Step Nine.

The second problem was not as easy to brush off. There is one key difference between every episode of *Fun House* you've ever seen and the one that lies in a vault at ITV – the toxicity levels of the gunge.

The first I knew something was up was during a Cowboys and Indians-themed game in which gunge-filled balloons were chucked by contestants at their partners. It was a cracking concept and really called to mind Sergio Leone's immortal Spaghetti Westerns with Clint Eastwood. The only key difference is that I don't recall *The Man With No Name* ever yelling out mid-scene: 'Ah, fuck . . . my eyes . . . my eyes . . . please stop!'

I'm nothing if not a pro and instinctively sensed something was wrong. My suspicions were confirmed when I went over to investigate and the lad in question's eyes looked as though they'd been attacked with a machete of some kind. Something told me this was not 'a whole lot of fun' even if there were still 'prizes to be won'.

The nameless boy (Michael Coburn) exited the studio in an ambulance while I did a tight fifteen-minute set about nose-picking to entertain the crowd. My heart wasn't really in it and the lacklustre reception suggested I wasn't the only one concerned with the wellbeing of our contestant.

The simple fact is that no child should be blinded during the recording of a television programme but these things happen. In this life, you learn from your mistakes. We picked ourselves up off the floor, found a new gunge supplier, and the stuff we covered the kids with, like the show itself, became non-toxic.

Other errors in that original version were less serious but more costly. We naïvely assumed that the central hook wasn't enough to keep people interested. Sometimes, you just have to back yourself and realise you're on to a winner but it's not always easy during the early stages of a new project. The actual Fun House – the concluding section of *Fun House* – is iconic now but we had no idea if it would catch on, so we made sure the prizes on offer were truly extraordinary. We lost a fortune on five-star holidays to New York and Fabergé eggs that day. Even now, I have no idea how they secured an original Monet but the red team can count themselves very lucky indeed (and not only because they escaped with only minor injuries).

If, miraculously, you're waiting with bated breath to hear if the pilot was successful then I can now, as my agent said when we parted company four months ago, put you out of your misery. The show was picked up. I had to wait a full week for the phone call to come but I was never worried. I spent the week daydreaming of games and gunge and glory and gaining a foothold in the children's presenting game. In fact, I was so sure that when the call came I answered immediately, 'So when do we start filming?' I had actually answered the previous fifteen phone calls that way, which confused many, including friends, family and Neil Buchanan, but the executives didn't know that and so, to them, it still sounded super cool.

I breathed a contented sigh, looked at the setting sun and considered what we were going to create, the joy and happiness that we were about to impart on the world. I muttered a favoured Kant quotation to myself: 'Morality is not the doctrine of how we may make ourselves happy, but how we may make ourselves worthy of happiness.' Then I added, 'This really is gonna be a whole lot of fun with prizes to be won.'

Chapter 11

Jimi Jamison – *Baywatch* Theme

It's hard to hear this song and not picture that magnificent chest bouncing up and down in slow motion. Dave Hasselhoff has never openly admitted to using conditioner on his chest hair, but to me it's screamingly obvious in that iconic, sexy opening sequence. Such a scene stealer.

Spending that time in Scotland really opened my eyes to the world around me. I've always felt that foreigners have their own ways of doing things and, with that spirit of embracing new, welcoming and good-humoured cultures, I set off for Germany and a whole new adventure.

I still appreciate how fortunate I was at that time. The pilot was a success; the show was happening and clearly bound for glory but I had a couple of weeks before we began filming while the gunge lawsuit was taken care of. It meant that I had the freedom of a young man to roam the globe seeking adventure but with the security of knowing I would be returning to my place as a made man in British television. This was a huge step. I still distinctly remember standing in my shower and thinking how important it was to remain grounded. Once I'd finished wiring the shower, I thought about how important it was to not let my imminent surge in fame go to my head.

Watching children fall over was clearly going to be the main focus of my life from that point but I was never going to forget the power of music and the need to share my DJing talent with the world. For that reason, I really wanted to get back to basics so I loaded up the boot of my Ford Cortina with a bunch of 7in records and went off to bring them, and more importantly my announcing and back-announcing of them, to the world.

Originally, I had simply stuck a pin in a map at random but, because so much of the earth's surface is water, fate kept trying to send me to the middle of an ocean of some sort and I gave up on that strategy and decided to go with my gut.

I'd heard good things about Germany but I still couldn't tell you exactly why I wanted to go there. In retrospect, it seems obvious: denim; mullets; a rich storytelling tradition; world-leading pop music of a very specific and not universally popular type; sausages . . . but at the time I really didn't give it that much thought. It just felt right.

I drove through France without a care in the world, stopping frequently to eat and drink and answer questions about my hair. The inhabitants of the sleepy towns I drifted through had never seen anything like it and insisted on plying me with wine while I told them about backcombing and the use of lemon juice to work as a natural highlight. 'If life gives you lemons, make subtle but effective accentuation of your tips,' I told Jean-Pierre, but he didn't seem to understand. Now I knew why the textbooks in school had suggested it was better to stick with asking directions to the discotheque and I often wonder if I'd even have got into this line of work if it wasn't for those early lessons.

The language was often a bit of a barrier but thankfully humanity runs deeper than our linguistic habits. There are things that bind us that we can forever share and it was a real joy to discover what those things were with my temporary French friends. One of them is obviously hair and the other 'Ça Plane Pour Moi' by Plastic Bertrand. We stood, arm in arm, and shouted out the lyrics but it was the music that ran deep, forging the bond between us. Music travels so much deeper than language. We were literally bellowing the following:

That's cool with me, me, me, me, me
That's cool with me
Hou! Hou! Hou! Hou!
That's cool with me

Even now, as I copy and paste those lyrics and alter the spacing, font and colour to bring them in line with the rest of this book, there are tears in my eyes. Linguistically, it's nonsense, but musically it's as pure a human experience as there could be. I bared my soul to the good people of France and, to quote the Google translation of that other French superstar, 'I have not regrets.'

By now, you've probably realised that hair is an important part of my life. In many ways, it has made me and, as you'll read in a couple of chapters' time, it has very nearly broken me. Cutting should be kept to a stylish minimum and shaving should be avoided at all costs. The way that this philosophy has been adopted on the continent is probably why I felt so at ease there and, for a while, I felt that France might be my spiritual home. That was until I got to Germany.

As soon as I crossed the border from the Netherlands, I froze. I'm not a superstitious man because I believe it's bad luck, but I have long been fascinated by the concept of the doppelganger. They say that when you see yours, then your days are numbered. I suppose mortality means that our days are all numbered anyway, but I think the suggestion is that the number is significantly reduced. There are many different theories on the doppelganger, but none of them are positive. Edgar Allan Poe wrote about its challenge to one's psychological equilibrium; Dostoevsky used the concept in a tale of a man having his character flaws exploited and life subsequently taken over by this eerie imposter; but it is the belief of many traditions that the 'double-ganger' is an omen of death that has always chilled me. Incidentally, it would be remiss of me not to thank Right Said Fred for turning me on to a lot of that Russian literature. I find it impossible to not think of Dostoevsky's *The Idiot* whenever I hear 'Deeply Dippy' and I'm sure I'm not the only one.

I only saw him from behind but he had the desert boots, he had the denim but, most of all, he had the *hair*. It was full, it was lustrous, it was bouncing around below the nape of his neck. It was mine. So convinced was I that I was looking at me, that I gave myself a bit of a start when I reached up and felt my own hair. The man turned around and I could see that it wasn't me but, no sooner had I relaxed a bit, I saw me on the other side of the street and then further up the street and then another four times in a shoe shop. I pulled over to rub my eyes and take some deep breaths. The world was spinning and it took quite a long time for it to stop. Years later, when I saw *Being John Malkovich* and it got to the moment when the actor enters a portal into his own brain, the memories came flooding back.

Once the world finally did stop spinning, I had a great time. I could have felt threatened by the powerful barnets on show but, instead, I was inspired. I spoke to my brothers through the universal language of hair, '99 Luftballons' by Nena and English. Cologne being a reasonably-sized city meant there were plenty of bilingual people.

At first, I did the DJ equivalent of busking. With my little record player and speakers, I found a corner of a leafy park and launched into a live broadcast as if I was safely tucked up in the BBC studios. It was an exhilarating experience. As I've already said, I'd done some outside broadcasts and thrived on the experience of being out there among the listeners, but this was a whole new level. With those broadcasts you still have big trucks and kit and banners and it's very obvious what you are and what's going on. In the Rheinpark, armed with only modest kit and my even more modest wits, I could easily have been mistaken for a madman, and I was on several occasions. The misunderstandings were quickly cleared up and it wasn't long before an al fresco disco (an al disco) was under way. It made me so happy. Once you reach a certain level of fame, you can begin to doubt yourself. Are they enjoying the work of the DJ or are they enjoying listening to Pat Sharp? Am I merely preaching to the converted? Those doubts drifted away on the wind along with the strains of 'Rush Hour' by Jane Wiedlin.

For those of you unfamiliar with Cologne, it's over in the west of Germany and, of course, back in 1989 that was more than a piece of simple geography. I really wasn't thinking about the political situation when I decided to go to Germany but it all fits into place when you look back on it. *Of course* that's what I was drawn to. Bringing people together is important, breaking down walls and, without wanting to overstate what I bring to the table as a DJ, by playing music with cheery links I do my part to make every single person in the country united.

The original Band Aid was still relatively fresh in my memory and, even now, I remember the effect it had on me and the goosebumps it gave me. Younger readers have probably read about those concerts and what they achieved, but I'll never forget the electricity and excitement as they were happening. It was an absolute privilege to watch Freddie Mercury performing at Wembley and, when it was over, I took a moment before turning off the TV and going to put the kettle on. I didn't know what I wanted to do, but I knew that I wanted to do something to help the world. It turns out that thing was unifying Germany.

I loved my time in Cologne and it was with a heavy heart that I left for Berlin. The weight around my ticker was probably to do with the sausages, pretzels and beer producing a thick insulating layer of fat but I had a young man's metabolism and, by the time I reached the capital, I felt spry once more.

I had met David Hasselhoff on a couple of occasions. He was always friendly and had that ability to fill rooms and hearts with happiness with his booming voice and powerful charisma. As I neared the west side of the Wall, there was a powerful optimism in the air. People were excited but there was still tension. It was a bit like the time we threw a surprise birthday party for Timmy Mallet. It was a lot like that, actually, as both saw a lot of smashing of walls.

I saw Dave from about a hundred yards away and you can still feel his aura from that distance. I thought there was a decent chance he'd know who I was, but I wasn't sure he'd remember our meetings. He did.

'Patman! Get yourself over here. You ever get that mustard stain out of your shirt? Oh, wait, that was just the shirt itself!' The yellow splodges on my blue shirt had caused Dave endless amusement when I wore it to Andrew Ridgeley's birthday party. We hugged and then stood with an arm over each other's shoulders and patted each other on the chest vigorously. The spring of that man's chest hair is like nothing you've ever known. If his chest were a mattress, it would never need flipping.

'Look at the two of us!' Dave bellowed and everybody nearby did as he said. 'With Patman's magnificent head of hair and my glorious chest hair, by our powers combined we're going to get something special done here!' There was a tremendous cheer and the excitement began to relieve the tension.

A lot of people remember Dave singing from on top of the Wall, but not many people remember that I announced and back-announced him. I spent a lot of time planning what I was going to say. Dave won't mind me saying that his German popularity far outweighed his British. That meant that introducing him was an entirely different beast. It meant that I could be more playful. There was more flexibility because the crowd were so knowledgeable about him. For a time, I had made up my mind to go with 'And now, ladies and gentleman, boys and girls, Damen und Herren, Jungen und Mädchen, a man who needs no introduction . . .' and leaving it there. I changed my mind, though. Even with all of his gold records in Germany and universal acclaim and adoration, I thought that gag might be a tough one for Dave to follow. In the end, I adopted the 'less is more' approach.

The good thing about live broadcasting is that you can get away with a lot more. Obviously, innuendo is the gift that keeps on giving to the DJ or presenter, but it is nice to be a bit more explicit from time to time. With that in mind, I had come up with the line, 'And now, the man who puts the ass in Hasselhoff!' but as I say, I had gone for a minimalist approach, whereby I simply screamed Dave's name. I couldn't shake the ass line from my head, though, and very nearly dropped it in during the instrumental section of 'Let It Be Me' but, as I saw him up there in those leather trousers, bending over and wiggling his bum, I thought it was too poignant a moment to shout out and get the laugh.

Occasionally, I go back and watch the footage of him up there on that Wall. It was a few days after the Wall started to come down and, watching it now, you can still see the raw humanity of the performance. There is hope, elegance, unity, the tying together of souls that Man had attempted to tear asunder and the majesty of the will of the people overcoming the arbitrary political shackles that attempted to quash love and the interconnectivity of humanity. I can't think of a better image to capture that than Dave up there with a leather jacket covered in flashing lights and a piano-keyboard tie. Dave was used to bringing the house down in Germany, but I know the highlight of his career was when he brought the Wall down. Other people were obviously involved, but you know what I mean.

I don't think there's anything that we can compare that moment to. The closest thing would be when Cliff Richard entertained the crowds at Wimbledon the time when it rained but I don't think it was quite the same. Obviously, the crowd was delighted to be reunited with the match between Goran Ivanisevic and Jason Stoltenberg, but I don't think it had quite the same resonance as being reunited with family members that you haven't seen for years. Even if they were serving up considerably fewer aces.

During my time, I was able to speak to quite a few of the people who had been estranged for a while. It was very powerful and impossible not to be moved – the police were constantly shepherding us all over the place, but I was able to stay in the same place for long enough to hear all about Christian's story. There were tears in his eyes and I asked him how long it had been since he'd seen his family. He was so choked up that he could barely speak but, eventually, he was able to collect himself and keep it together just enough to be able to get the words out.

'Four days,' he said.

Christian had gone to college in a nearby town and just popped back to be at this monumental moment with his family. They didn't actually know anybody from the east.

'Sorry, the dust from the Wall is getting into my eyes and catching in the back of my throat,' he told me with an earnestness and haunting dignity that I'll never forget.

I still can't quite believe I was there when it happened. I feel deeply honoured and privileged to have been so. A lot of people ask me what I took away from that experience and the answer is a whole bunch of ideas for *Fun House*. You will have noticed lots of destruction, things falling over and so on. We also had the contestants divided when they went into the Fun House one by one so that we could have the joy when they were reunited at the end, ready to collect their bounty of mid-priced electronics and books with a token educational element.

I had watched one of the most iconic moments of the twentieth century but now it was time to get back home and create some of my very own.

Chapter 12

Deep Blue Something – 'Breakfast at Tiffany's'

I've always loved BaT. It's witty and light, beautifully written and with one of the most alluring, enigmatic characters of all time. Quite why some clown decided to turn 4 minutes and 20 seconds of pop perfection into a whole book is beyond me.

They say that if you remember the '90s you weren't really there but they're just being playful. I can remember that glorious decade in poignant, excruciating detail and there are hundreds of hours of recorded footage of my being there. There were lots of people in the '90s and I think the vast majority remember being there.

It was such an exciting time and the colours of the clothes were so vibrant. I remember trotting along to Manchester to spend a night in the Hacienda. The music was as loud as the tie-dye t-shirts and I remember the thumping in my ears would last for days afterwards. Those nights were always so joyous. Everybody was having a great time, hugging each other, smiling, dancing and, as a man who doesn't drink, it was so refreshing to see people not getting drunk. I was able to go and get a lemonade and lime from the bar whenever I wanted with absolutely no risk of a queue. I don't think I've ever felt so loved. People I hadn't even met would hug me and tell me what I meant to them. Thinking about it now is making me a little misty-eyed.

On top of that, people were handing out sweets all over the place. My sugary drink was enough for me so I never took part but the amount of Tic Tacs I saw flying around was crazy. I remember those adverts where the woman with the nice teeth said that each Tic Tac was just one calorie. Amazing to think people got enough of a sugar hit off that to dance until 8.00am the next morning.

The early '90s was such an amazing time for music. The spirit of the era was probably best summed up by The Shamen with their number-one hit 'Ebeneezer Goode' and its glorious refrain: 'Es are good . . . Es are good . . . he's Ebeneezer Goode.'

That chorus was controversial at the time but I still don't know why. It was clear to me that the song was basically doing for British culture what *Sesame Street* had done on American TV for decades; championing the merits of one of the great letters and aiding its appeal to children. K will always have my heart but E is certainly worthy of having its profile raised. Also, the name Ebeneezer is clearly no coincidence and I have it on good authority that Charles Dickens was a huge influence on a lot of those acid house lads. Rumour has it the name of the genre was taken from the working title of *Bleak House*.

Like acid house, my fame was steadily rising during this period. Using public transport was impossible without people constantly coming over for a chat or getting me to sign stuff, which was why I opted for this mode of travel whenever possible. I was interviewed in magazines, presenting (what I felt was) the nation's favourite television programme and being invited to all the right parties. Life was good. Ebeneezer Goode.

One such party was hosted by Simon Fowler of Ocean Colour Scene. Simon is and was a lovely bloke but he's one of those people adamant that everyone should be able to get on. He's never diplomatic when sorting a guest list and will just invite all his mates, regardless of what they think of each other. He didn't care if you were Yitzhak Rabin and Yasser Arafat, under his roof he expected civility. And when they didn't provide it, they were asked to leave.

I'll never forget arriving at his plush home in Maida Vale that fateful night and being informed that Liam Gallagher and Damon Albarn were both in attendance. At first, it was fine, Damon was in the kitchen browsing the cereal selection and Liam was in one of the bedrooms discussing *Madame Bovary* with Zoe Ball. I was the only person who seemed to be concerned about the powder keg in the party and that, like the milk in Simon's fridge, it was about to go off. Damon was actually about to find Simon and alert him to this fact about the milk, saying: 'These Golden Grahams are OK, but I don't think he'll get away with this milk in the morning.' I grabbed him to stop him leaving the kitchen, which was a bit awkward at first but I turned it into a hug and then a light foxtrot, which Damon really got into. By the time we received the adulation of the kitchen, he'd forgotten all about trying to find Simon.

I darted upstairs to check on the Liam situation and bumped into him on the stairs. Apparently, when asked if Emma Bovary's attempt to find meaning in a string of affairs was always doomed, he had answered, 'Does Flaubert shit in the woods?' and rightly left the room immediately. He was on his way to grab a bowl of cereal (how similar these two warring popstars really were) so obviously I had to intercept. I went for the hug and foxtrot combo but it was ill-advised on the stairs. 'Get off me, you knob,' said Liam, 'the stairs is no place for dancing and the music is clearly not in 4/4 time so a foxtrot is not suitable.' I panicked and took one for the team. I took a deep breath and said, 'Is it true that Noel writes all the best stuff?'

I got a black eye and a damaged eardrum from the screaming but the worst thing was that this diversion tactic only bought us an hour. The two ended up bumping into each other in the queue for the toilet and it all went as badly as any of us could have expected.

Minutes later and Liam was apparently bawling his eyes out in the bedroom while Damon was sat on the floor of the loo telling half of Kula Shaker that he knew he shouldn't have come and he wished he'd never been born.

I knew I had to step in. I'm not sure why, possibly it's my extensive experience working with children, but I've always been a great peacemaker. My wife has often said I'd make a great hostage negotiator in another life but if we get a few goes at this crazy little thing called life, like Buddhists and cats believe, then I'd rather keep doing what I'm doing – something worthwhile.

I let Liam run his fingers through my hair for half an hour before distracting Damon with some devastating wordplay – 'How's your night been? A blur?' – and we just about got away with it. Although I later learned the pair had a drunken punch-up in the garden minutes after I left. Brett Anderson from Suede was the collateral damage and ended up in hospital with mild concussion. You can't win them all. You just have to enjoy the ones you do win.

I used to joke on air that Britpop was just how I referred to Tizer (until the station manager told me the gag was getting tiresome). While I'd seen a few of the lads involved at parties, it wasn't until the 1996 Brit Awards and Jarvis Cocker wiggling his bum during Michael Jackson's performance that I realised quite how serious all this was.

It started, as these things tend to, innocently enough. I was presenting the award for Best Soundtrack (*Batman Forever*, although I maintain that *Muriel's Wedding* was robbed). The event took place at Earl's Court and it seemed to go on for ever. It was like the Neil Buchanan sections of *ZZZap!*. Presenters and musicians alike started to drink a bit more than was perhaps sensible (in my case strawberry Nesquik, easily the best option, whatever you might hear from Jimmy Nail and the rest of the 'chocolate truthers'). We played cards for an hour or two but then somebody suggested a game of 'Truth or Dare' and things escalated.

I should have known things were going to spiral after an awkward moment with the Pet Shop Boys. I'd always got on well with Neil Tennant but he wasn't in the greatest mood that night, no doubt exacerbated by my insistence that he do some shots and screaming, 'Stop *being boring*!' in his face every time he refused. I felt this was a solid bit of wordplay but he found it threatening in the extreme.

Anyone with an even cursory knowledge of Neil's back catalogue would have known that 'truth' was never going to be an issue for a man who'd written some truly confessional lyrics. Instead, I opted for 'dare' and it was time to either go big or go home. The Pet Shop Boys were notorious at the time for their downbeat and understated live shows so I said, 'I dare you and

Chris to wear something more adventurous than your usual jeans and tatty old t-shirts at your next gig.' I've no idea if they actually went through with it but hopefully I can make it along to one of their concerts at some point and find out.

It was a rare occasion when I drank so much that I was genuinely out of control. Thinking about my encounter with Alanis Morissette at that awards ceremony still makes me cringe whenever I think of it, more often than not in a cold sweat in the middle of the night. I'd been on the Nesquik but also had a couple of sugary teas so was on quite the sugar high. The Canadian songstress was there to pick up her award for Best International Breakthrough Act and sing her latest single, 'Hand in My Pocket'. She walked offstage with the contented smile that follows a job well done and I hissed, 'One hand in your pocket? That's a good one – I've never once seen you get your round in.' It is quite clear that we don't mature so much as get bigger. The strange thing was that the meaner I treated her, the keener she became. I hope I'm not speaking out of school when I say that Alanis was all over me that night and the look on her face when I introduced her to my beautiful wife is not something I forgot in a hurry. She vented her frustration to a waiter in a long rant about there being a fly in her wine.

A bigger problem, and not for the first time, was Mick Hucknall. Huck was really keen to be involved in the fun even though we did our best to ignore him. Gary Barlow, one of the youngest lads present, insisted nobody should be left out and made a space for him in the circle. It was a lovely gesture but was undercut somewhat when Mick selected 'dare' and Gary said, 'Pull one of your teeth out.'

Sometimes at night, I can almost smell that heady combination of blood and vomit. Still, fair play to the Huckster, his performance of 'Fairground' that night was nothing short of exemplary and I believe deserves to be considered the equal of that German goalkeeper who played on with a broken neck.

Jarvis was always a real laugh at those events and you knew that if he knocked back enough hooch he'd do just about anything. With that in mind, I dared him to interrupt Jacko's set. My exact words were, 'Go on, make an arse of yourself.' I think he may have misheard me or simply taken the whole thing too literally because the next thing I knew his bum was causing a major diplomatic incident. That turned out to be Jacko's penultimate performance in the UK before his passing and I can't help but feel partly responsible that we didn't get to see more of the man on these shores. On the other hand, it was funny, as a wiggled bum so often is.

I've been lucky enough to go to the Brits a lot over the past few years and got to know a lot of people in the music industry. It works a lot like school years where you're obviously closest to the people from your 'year', but I've had some fun times with some talented folk from the years below. One that I remember particularly well was young Peter Doherty. We were on the same table and had some great chats about our favourite comedies from the 1950s. It spilled over and he invited me back to his place for an after-party. I had no idea that little Pete was diabetic but, no sooner were we in the flat than he pulled out his insulin needle and took a much needed top-up. I didn't think that insulin was supposed to be administered intravenously but he'd know better than me. What was so nice was that even though we didn't know each other that well, he was so relaxed in my company that he didn't even bother to speak and fell into a deep sleep while moaning pleasurably.

The year after the Jarvis affair was all about Spicemania. It's hard to imagine now but any young women reading this need to realise that the Spice Girls actually invented feminism with their début album in 1996. The pity is that they only released three records – I have no doubt that if they'd been as prolific as Bob Dylan, then Hillary Clinton would have become President without any issues.

There was controversy in '97 even before the event began. Liam Gallagher, who'd obviously completely forgotten my pep talk in Maida Vale, said he wouldn't attend the Brits because if he bumped into the Spice Girls, he would smack them. It was a classic bit of violent frivolity from the Oasis man but the recent invention of feminism meant that we now realised the idea of hitting women actually wasn't all that hilarious. The ladies had the last laugh, however, when they received the award for Best British Video and Sporty challenged Liam with the immortal words, 'Come and have a go if you think you're hard enough.' Better still, the best revenge is living well and she got to do a duet with Bryan Adams soon after.

I was excited by the Spice Girls and what they were doing, not least this wonderful movement they'd started which I liked to refer to as 'first-wave feminism'. The girls liked me, too – largely for the hair tips, admittedly – but I think our bond went beyond that. There was only one major bone of contention between us and that concerned their nicknames: Scary, Sporty, Baby, Ginger and Posh. If I told them once, I told them a thousand times – only one of those is actually a spice (ginger). I told the offenders to go with Cumin, Paprika, Coriander and

Cinnamon but they weren't having any of it. Maybe the innuendo possibilities presented by Cumin put them off, but any DJ
worth his salt would prefer that to Baby.

If the 1997 Brit Awards are remembered for anything, it's for
me presenting the Best British Producer award to John Leckie.
If they're remembered for a second thing, it's Geri Halliwell's
Union Jack dress. Spicemania was at its height in the UK and
the Spice Girls had just cracked the US as well, reaching Number
1 with their début single and album. Ginger Spice, as the only
one with an acceptable nickname, rightly became a symbol of
the zeitgeist and the pin-up girl for Cool Britannia, a feminist
icon perved over by lonely teenage boys up and down the
country. Geri's a lovely girl and she deserved all of that but my
role in proceedings has never been known by the public at
large. Until now.

I was standing backstage with the girls about an hour before
they were due to go on. Four of them were doing vocal warm-
ups while Posh sat on her own in the corner nonchalantly
chewing gum. They all looked stunning, as ever, but Geri was
wearing an American flag, those iconic stars and stripes. I pulled
her to one side and said, 'Ginger, darling, I don't know much
but I'm fairly sure horizontal stripes make you look fatter.'

She looked utterly crestfallen and just started repeating the
word 'shit' over and over again like a mantra. She managed to
find an all-black dress and Mark Morrison, sensing the gravity
of the situation, emerged from the kitchen with a Union Jack
tea-towel. That was good of him, especially when reoffending
could have landed him back in prison so soon after being
released. You reap what you sew and Gabrielle truly earned her
title of Best British Female that night with an incredible bit of

needlework (ironic as *Trainspotting* got Best Soundtrack, but everyone told me to shut up when I pointed this out at the time). All the more impressive since I'm still not entirely sure how many eyes Gabrielle has.

Later on that evening, Geri thanked me for my advice and said she was thinking about slipping into something a bit more comfortable for the remainder of the evening. I thought this was an excellent idea and told her, 'You just need to focus on being comfortable now . . . the looser the better.' To this day, I have no idea where she found that red dress but I couldn't help but feel partially responsible – as well as vaguely aroused – when her nipple popped out.

The apotheosis of Cool Britannia was probably Euro '96 the previous summer. It seemed like every window was draped with an England flag in a way that didn't feel racist. There was such a great feeling around the country that summer and I know that was at least partly because of the imminence of series eight of *Fun House*. I actually went to the semi-final against Germany and I fondly recall walking through the streets around Wembley singing songs at the top of my lungs that gently ribbed England's opponents. I turned a corner and was confronted with a group of terrifying German men with faces like thunder. They'd obviously heard my chants. Not for the first time, I wondered where all my mates were. I could almost taste the vomit in my mouth and the noises my stomach was making made it clear that that chocolate milkshake had been a mistake. And I don't say that lightly.

They saw me and they saw the hair. The ringleader looked me up and down and his frown turned, quite literally, upside down. He walked over slowly, put his arms around my chest and gave me a hug that would comfortably find a place in my all-time Top 10. There were about fifteen of them and they took it in turns to cuddle me. I don't know if they knew about *Fun House*, my Berlin Wall heroics or were just pleased to see a Londoner with a mullet, but something special happened that night. I remember thinking that I just wanted all of this to last for ever.

But things don't last for ever. Not even *The NeverEnding Story*. England lost that night, Blur, Oasis and the Spice Girls would all split up within a few years and *Fun House*, having found its feet after a decade on the air, was inexplicably axed in its prime. But that's a whole other story.

Chapter 13

Shampoo – 'Trouble'

Something certainly came along and it burst my bubble. It's hard to listen to this song without wincing but it's a masterpiece. You don't follow 'Incredible' by M Beat featuring General Levy on Now 29 *unless you're a little bit special.*

The end of *Fun House* was obviously a huge event in my life but, before I tell you about it, I feel you need to know a bit more about me. You've heard about the good stuff – the talent, the presenting, the Haircut 100 gag. You also need to hear about the bad stuff and one bad thing in particular. It's a risk to bare one's soul but it would be dishonest to release this book and edit out the darkness so that you only see the successful television and radio personality. Plus, I've been told it could help sales.

You may have expected to see the word 'hair' in that list of my positive attributes (it actually is contained within Haircut 100 if you look closely . . . but that's not the point). Perhaps it should have been there but, just as Samson's hair was both his strength and his weakness, so is mine. I, too, had my Delilah and she went by the name 'addiction'.

To start this story, I need to take you back to school – and not in the way that some people use as a cuss to suggest that they are about to educate you but in a shameful or humiliating way to belittle you – but because it was an afternoon when I was in school that this all started.

I needed to go to the toilet for the usual reasons but, as I got close to the door, I began to hear odd noises. There were hushed tones and lots of shuffling. Part of me wanted to turn away and I wonder how my life would have turned out if I had. A good rule of thumb when you're young and at school is never to run away from anything. If bullies can tease you for being scared of something, they will, and the more ridiculous that thing is, the funnier they will find it and the more it will stick. 'Pat is scared of the toilet!' I assume they'd have said; 'I hope there isn't a urinal anywhere because Pat will freak out . . .' they would probably have cried; 'Pat probably won't come in tomorrow . . . he'll need to poo and get so scared in the toilet that he'll keep pooing and be in a vicious circle for ever . . .' one of the more creative bullies would no doubt have announced. So I didn't run. I went in. I saw some of the bigger boys and I caught them in the middle of something.

They were all trying to cram into one of the cubicles but there wasn't enough room, meaning Joe Gribbins was sticking out. He was the one who turned and caught my eye and that was when I knew I was in deep.

'What you looking at, Sharp?'

There are countless good comebacks to this question but none of them come to mind when you're in that situation fearing for both your immediate safety and the rest of your school career. I was mute, the silent, dead air lasting long enough for the emergency automated announcement to have kicked in if we'd been broadcasting.

'Not going to tell anyone are you, Sharp?' asked Paul Coombes as the rest of the group moved menacingly out of the cubicle and into the main body of the room.

'What are you doing?' I asked, backing away even though I had no intention of running.

'Got some gear off my big brother,' said Sam Peters with a mischievous grin. 'He got some for a party he's having and gave me some to have a go.' Sam sniffed and rubbed his nose. 'You going to tell on us, Sharp?'

I froze, knowing that as much as my word is my bond, it looked like they wouldn't let their secret out of these toilets alive.

'I asked you a question, Sharp.'

I stammered my clumsy response of 'no' and shook my head. The others all laughed.

'I think there's only one way to trust him,' said Paul who was eyeing me up and down. 'Give him some, too. That way he's incriminated with the rest of us.'

The others cheered and I felt hands on my collar. I was shoved into the cubicle and made to kneel before the toilet. The lid was closed and there was a small container in the centre. 'That stuff is expensive, so don't take too much. You don't need a lot anyway,' said Sam from behind. Trembling, I took the container and scooped out a small amount of the strange substance into the palm of my hand. I was praying that a teacher would walk in at any moment. This felt like one of those defining moments like in the exemplary Gwyneth Paltrow vehicle *Sliding Doors* (although it would have been a different reference point in my head at the time since the film hadn't yet been released). In that moment, I'd rather have had endless detentions than potentially tread down a dark path. There was no respite, though, and I went through with it. 'Get it on your fingertips and just work it through gently,' Sam told me and then he handed me a comb. It was all a blur and I remember being moved to the mirror but I was too dazed and euphoric to focus properly on how I looked. That was it, though. The beginning of my affair with hair products. My a-hair.

The use of gels and waxes was banned in school so we had to tread a fine line, whereby we used enough stuff to make our hair look outstanding but not so much that it was obvious that there was a lot of product in there. I used to meet Sam, Paul and the others every day for some follicle finessing. One day, Sam was putting the finishing touches to a masterful quiff when he told me that there was to be no gel for me. 'You've got to contribute, mate. You're a good lad and you've got a sick 'do, but you're not going to keep getting freebies.' I was crestfallen. It wasn't that I was being cut off (although that was pretty painful), it was that I hadn't even considered what a sponge I'd been. I needed to make it up to the guys, but how, when I had no income of my own?

I'm not proud of this, but I stole from my mum. Perhaps she knows more than I realise but I suspect that reading this is the first time she'll learn about it. Mum was a big hairspray fan so, to start with, I would just take the cans from the bathroom. Why would she suspect? There was one time when she saw me walking with a can.

'Why have you got my hairspray?' she asked sweetly, completely oblivious to the fact that she was witnessing a crime.

'Oh, is this hairspray? I thought it was lunch.' I uttered these words with an ease and conviction that would put a hardened criminal to shame.

'Silly thing,' Mum said as I stood there suddenly aware of the deception of which I was capable.

Things went smoothly for a while but I hit trouble after a couple of months. 'More hairspray, Sharp? You know that this is designed for voluminous curly hair when none of us have that type. One of the subconscious foundations of our friendship is a collective experience of having fine hair. Get some proper gel or wax would you?'

I'm not sure why, but stealing money felt worse than stealing hairspray. I suppose it's the same thing as taking Post-it notes or pens from work. That's not really stealing, whereas it would be if you took money or somebody's shoes. However, as everyone knows, if you take absolutely loads of money and people's pensions, then it, of course, goes back to being as trivial as Post-its.

I'd like to say that there was a great story in this and a strong moral lesson . . . but there isn't. On several occasions, I went into my mum's purse and took money. I spent that money on hair products and was never caught.

By the time I was working at Radio 1, I was deep into the hair game. There was nothing I didn't know about mousses and shampoos and how to get the most out of each hair and its constituent medullas, cortexes and cuticles. I wasn't quite at the level of fame where people simply bring hair products to you, so I was still buying stuff off the streets.

I think that I knew I was addicted but, for some reason, it didn't trouble me. I put it down to the way that you feel like you're bulletproof at that age. I was just having a good time. I was a man with a head full of keratin and a heart full of adventure. Looking back, I was reckless and not just because I would wash my hair upwards of once a day, putting more trust in man-made chemicals than my hair's natural oils. When you move into the world of celebrity, you get sucked into a whole new dimension of excess. Most people know what it's like to be at a house party where the booze is flying in from every direction, but not everybody knows what it's like to be at a party where that booze costs £15,000 a bottle. It was the same with hair. I'd go to parties where I'd end up washing my hair five times with undiluted Moroccan oil. I got a taste for it. I knew that I was doing lasting damage to the roots and that I was interfering with the hair's natural process of self-conditioning, but I loved that rush so much. I wasn't thinking about consequences, I was thinking about the nourishing properties of arran kernels mixed with pomegranate seeds for extra antioxidising benefits. I defy anyone to be confronted by Sonia, a bowl of warm water and a tablespoon of sweet-smelling, deep orange nectar and not go in for a deep wash. I'll always remember re-entering the room after a quick blow-dry and being met by silent reverence. Limahl from Kajagoogoo quipped that he wasn't sure which was more beautiful, my hair or the silence. Sonia appeared to take it well but was noticeably quieter afterwards.

One of the worst aspects of all this was the sheer number of occasions when beautiful women would run their fingers through my hair for hours on end and yet have no interest in a word I had to say. It was pure objectification and they liked me only for my hair's natural lustre. In fact, they didn't like me at all and it sometimes felt as though my hair was the ladies' man and I was just the irritating appendage beneath it.

Looking back, I could have got myself into some trouble. It was clear that a lot of the characters shifting stuff were a bit shady but I thought nothing of wandering into dark alleys and approaching men with trench coats. The worst thing that ever happened was seeing a coat opened to reveal a shrivelled penis rather than a selection of high-end hair products. That happened several times and I never screamed, neither did I laugh. I simply maintained eye contact and gave a sympathetic and slightly sad smile. On every single occasion, the man (it was never the same one) let his shoulders sink an inch or two and met my gaze with a poignant flicker that gave me hope for them. I honestly think it helped. There is great power in eye contact and I really do think so in mine especially. I actually think it's one of the reasons it was never possible for me to remain on radio for ever and eternally turn my back on television.

Most of the guys selling stuff on the streets were part of one gang or another. You learn pretty quickly whose turf is whose. Gels were largely the domain of the Guatemalans. If you were looking for more of a serum, then you went for the Peruvians. Then, of course, you had different parts of town belonging to different groups. You heard about shootings but I didn't witness any violence. I didn't ever see a gun, to be honest, but every single one of those guys had scissors. Most of them were thinning scissors or styling ones, though, so you'd be a fool to stab somebody and risk blunting an end. There were a lot of curling tongs knocking about, too, and I did hear stories of a guy having his ears and hands clamped in a pair. His ears and hands did not come out looking straight with a pleasing sheen. They came out looking blistered and very painful, apparently. That's a horrible thing to happen to you but, if you are so far into an enemy's turf that they have access to a plug socket, then you have to ask yourself some serious questions, I think.

I got along with everybody. I would use my presenting skills and ask people questions about themselves. I would use my hands and voice to generate enthusiasm and that meant these guys were happy to have me around. It is also fair to say that they all loved my hair. I may have relied on my hair a bit to give me my life but my hair relies even more heavily on me being alive to exist. They say there is honour among thieves, but there is also honour among hair. These guys knew mine was a work of art and they were happy to be a part of it, and be paid extremely well.

You would, of course, get people chancing their arm. I'm sorry to say that I've bought a bottle of what I thought was ultra-exclusive Ten Voss, only to get it home and find that it's actually a non-branded shampoo/conditioner two-in-one smuggled into a counterfeit bottle. A shampit or, as I prefer to think of it, a conpoo. I don't mind getting duped so much – fool me twice, shame on me, but for it to be a filthy hybrid rubs horrible salt into the wound. Thankfully, I didn't actually let any of the filth touch my hair. I was violently sick immediately after popping the cap.

The real problem that we don't address as a society is the danger of hair product abuse among the needy. You'll have no doubt seen homeless people, their clothes tattered and torn, their faces grubby and red and their hair greasy and lank. So very lank. They can only get their hands on non-branded, normally imported mousses and this, combined with rudimentary washing, means they are at extremely high risk of weakened cuticles, vitamin deficiencies and even bleaching. These people deserve a chance and I know they could turn their lives around with a return to their former hair glory. Formhair glory. We all know what we can achieve with just one good hair day.

Would Einstein have finalised his theory of relativity if he hadn't woken up with a perfect side parting that one time? I think we all know the answer. We need to be tough on poor hair products, tough on the causes of poor hair products.

I may not have run into trouble with the gangs, but I did have a bit of a run-in with the law. I'd popped to Paris for a weekend for romantic reasons and, on the way back, was hanging around in Calais. I went to one of those hypermarkets and was impressed by the size of the trolleys. People were stacking them with wine but I had no interest in doing the same. What I did have interest in was the tax-free hair products aisle. I went to town. I went to town, knocked on every door and became such an integral part of the town that the local council voted unanimously to give me a memorial bench in the park on the occasion of my death.

The car and brand-new trailer I'd bought to transport my bounty heaved itself off the ferry and I got to the Customs checkpoint. In my experience, being a celebrity in this situation can go one of two ways – you can either be waved through in exchange for an autograph as the officer is so desperate for you to like them that they want to cause you as little inconvenience as possible; or they can see this as their chance to spend some time with you and find out more about you. This particular officer did the latter and was very pleased to find some Murray Mints in my glove box. 'These are my favourite,' he said, beaming. I didn't have the heart to tell him that they had been brought by a passenger some months ago and did nothing for me. Instead, I looked at him kindly and maintained the illusion that the presence of this confectionery in some way made us the same.

You're probably aware that it's permissible to bring duty-free products in from France as long as they are for personal use. This is something of a grey area and it's largely accepted that, unless you are pushing your luck, you'll probably be fine. My guy here had a hard time believing this much product could be for my personal use. 'Your hair is perfect. Why would you need this stuff?' he asked, showing a lack of logical thinking that I knew was going to be a problem.

'To make it perfect,' I replied, with a positive cadence in my voice and waving my arms to generate enthusiasm. A technique that, until that point, had never failed me. It didn't fail that time either. I felt bad imparting that lesson and breaking his worldview but it's kinder that he knows and I really wanted to get home and get the sweet, sweet French spoils into my bathroom and some kind of storage facility. The man had, and I'm not trying to be unkind, deeply average hair. It wasn't bad by any means, but I could tell that he had accepted it. He knew his hair wasn't going to excel and had made peace with that. So what does he do when he sees somebody with high-end, superlative hair? He puts it down to genetics, to fate, to destiny, to luck. That isn't something he could ever achieve, so it isn't his fault that he doesn't. Yes, I have had help with good hair genes, but I still work hard at it, and he has no excuse for not working hard, too. I hope that these days he does.

Addiction is often thought of as a means of searching for something that is missing, to fill a gap that exists in one's soul. I think there's something in that and, as my fame grew, that gap did get a little bigger. Being in hair and make-up was where I began to feel happiest. I would be warm and fuzzy and any tension in my shoulders would ebb away. In retrospect, that was probably the fumes but I feel the point stands.

It was those same fumes, however, that led me to my darkest hour. *Fun House* was at the height of its considerable powers. I graced the pages of teen, gossip and glamour magazines. I was very, very good and my hair was majestic. I was untouchable and, because of the volume of stuff in it, my hair even more so. I headed up to Glasgow blissfully unaware of what was going to happen. I checked into my usual hotel room and practised my back-announcing for five hours until sleep overcame me. When I awoke, I still didn't realise that something was wrong. Very wrong.

Julia was the head of the eleven-person team who worked on my hair and although she is a professional and tried to hide her initial reaction as a way of protecting me, I could read her expression. I didn't know exactly what it was but I could guess.

'Why don't we pop you down and get you a coffee,' she said with a thin-lipped smile that confirmed to me what I feared most – split ends.

You will, of course, be aware of split ends and probably be quite accepting of them, which is very kind-hearted of you, but you're part of the problem as it's a poison. Split ends are to the presenter what damaged cruciate ligaments are to foot-ballers; it's what being caught stealing in Egypt is to pianists; it's what being Neil Buchanan is to Neil Buchanan. It's still too painful to retell this episode in great detail but I can tell you there were tears, there were tantrums, there were threats of violence and there were suicide attempts. I refused to go on as we pumped greater and greater volumes of everything we had at the top of my head to try and make this go away. We were fifty-two hours late starting the recording when the terrible thing happened.

Billy Gubb was a plump little child. I'm told he loved the show more than life itself and that he hadn't slept for four months since finding out he was going to be on. He'd been waiting for it to start for over fifty hours and, according to his mother, when he slipped into my hair and make-up room, it wasn't due to impatience or even to find out what was happening. Gubby just wanted to see if I was OK. He was dead by the time he reached the hospital. His little asthma-plagued lungs were overrun by the fumes in minutes and his body went into shock. As The Gubbster was being wheeled into the ambulance I took the stage, momentarily finding myself again and remembering what was important – a series of games based on pratfalls where children could win accessories they didn't need.

Gubby McGubbGubb was the greatest but not the only casualty. Years of substance abuse and that episode in particular caused lasting damage to my hair and I had to amputate the bottom 7in. The mullet was no more, but more on that later. I've never said or written this before but it's long overdue: 'Hi, I'm Pat Sharp . . . and I'm a hair products addict.'

I also did loads of cocaine in those years.

Chapter 14

Hanson – 'MMMBop'

Complex, wistful, harmonic, bittersweet, transcendental at times and as catchy as Shane Warne in the slips, this is probably my favourite Hanson track.

There is a story I love about the *Seinfeld* finale that I never tire of telling. The airing of the final episode on the west coast of the United States coincided with the death of Frank Sinatra. Sinatra's ambulance was able to arrive at his home and then rush him to hospital in light traffic largely because so many people in Los Angeles were indoors watching the show. Sinatra died anyway and the last *Seinfeld* is generally considered one of the biggest disappointments in television history, but that's beside the point. TV matters.

That eagerly awaited televisual farewell was broadcast in 1997 and, while it's probably overstating the case to suggest the world was watching when *Fun House* ended a couple of years later, it would be entirely accurate to suggest all of England was. I was totally focused on my job at the time so didn't get to see what the press were writing, but I can only assume they were speculating about what the finale had in store. Was it all a dream? Would I move to Paris? Would the 'will they/won't they?' sexual tension between myself and the twins finally be resolved?

Eventually, after hours of discussion and countless creative meetings, we decided to just do a normal episode. I bet Jerry Seinfeld wishes he'd thought of that.

It's hard to believe now, at a time when I would literally kill or shave my head to be back on telly on a regular basis, but I was actually getting quite bored by the end of the run. What people don't realise about *Fun House* is that it was actually quite a repetitive show. Oh yes, we could change the name of rounds or throw in some gunge when it wasn't expected, but those on the inside realised it was quite formulaic. There were times in the last year where I was phoning it in. It seems strange to me that the film *Gladiator* got so much press in 2001 when they computer-generated Oliver Reed after he died in the middle of filming, given that I was calling up the studio from home, doing my bit and they were superimposing my body in afterwards quite a few times that series. And I died a lot more times than Reedy while filming stuff! That was a little joke there, and apologies to any of his relatives if they happen to be reading this.

We are all the same. When you're young, you just assume you'll live for ever and present TV shows for kids while you're at it. But that's not the case. Whether I live for ever is like a transparent urn – remains to be seen. But one thing is for certain – *Fun House* did not last for ever.

In many ways, that home straight was a lot like a failing marriage. The spark was gone and the only answer was to try and come up with new and innovative ways of doing it to keep things fresh. Years before *Have I Got News for You* decided to have a rotating series of guest hosts, we did something similar. Obviously, we didn't mess with the presenter, that would have been counter-productive and borderline criminal, but we did experiment with guest directors. Most of the people we brought in were unknowns or guys who'd done some music videos but, one fine day, in September 1999, Mike Leigh agreed to come in and work on the show.

We were all thrilled with this coup, not least because the great man had recently made *Secrets and Lies* and *Topsy-Turvy*, and *Fun House* seemed like the obvious next step in his career. The show never aired but I have a LaserDisc copy in the living room. Watching it now, you can understand ITV's reservations. Here's a transcript of a typical section of that episode:

> Martina: (between puffs on a cigarette) I'm keeping it, Pat. That baby deserves a home.
> Melanie: Yeah, she's my sister and if she says she's keeping it, then I support her 100 per cent.
> Pat: Oh, sweetheart, you're breaking my heart.

It isn't until seventeen minutes into the episode that one of the rounds begins and, even when it does, both teams spend the bulk of it crying their eyes out. Even with the tremendous healing powers of time, it is a tough watch.

Yes, with hindsight this was a mistake. Or, if you're ITV, foresight. But there's an important point hidden among all those cigarettes, cups of tea and discussions about abortion. This will sound weird to you because you're not in the industry, but each show genuinely started to feel exactly the same. The same jokes, the same gunge, the same stilted conversations with teenagers. What the Mike Leigh experiment proved was that sometimes the very act of trying to revamp a thing is enough to remind you why you fell in love with it in the first place. Think of it like the plot of 'The Piña Colada Song', although without the entirely unnecessary dig at yoga.

I knew the writing was on the wall the day I bumped into Wolf from *Gladiators* in The Groucho Club. He asked me what I'd been up to and I replied, with a heavy heart, 'Oh, you know, same old, same old.' I asked him the same thing and his eyes lit up as he spoke about pushing over referee John Anderson. It didn't matter to the Wolfman that he'd done this hundreds of times before – he still had the passion that I was beginning to lack.

That wasn't the only warning sign. Around that time, I set up my own production company and began to develop my passion project (and by 'develop', as anyone involved in television knows, I mean drink coffee and talk about something for hours on end without any sign of an end product). I was adamant that combining entertainment for kids with education could be a winner. I felt that history and music made ideal bedfellows, and I even adapted the lyrics of Lou Bega's 'Mambo No. 5' so that it worked from the perspective of King Henry VIII. I was especially proud of my work having never even heard Mambos 1-4. The producers at *Fun House* were aghast at my suggestion that viewers could learn at the same time as being entertained, so I present the lyrics to 'Mambo No. VIII' below for public consumption for the very first time:

1, 2, 3, 4, 5 . . . I was married six times only one survived,
Divorce made me a church reformer,
One died of natural causes but I really didn't mourn
her,
Privy Council that I had was weak,
And when it came to wives I had a ruthless streak,

I liked Katherines, Aragon, Howard and Parr,
And a couple of Annes I admired from afar,
So what can I do? I begged the mighty Lord,
I need an heir but first a consort,
Anyone dry, it's all good, I'll still hump it,
But then to the block, send the strumpet.
A little less monasteries in my life,
A little bit of Wolsey by my side,
A little bit of wild boar and some mead,
A little bit of break from papacy,
A little bit of searching for a son,
A little Real Tennis all day long,
A little bit of death by beheading,
But my God-given right makes me your King.

Does it bother me that this never made it to air? Not in the slightest. Sometimes, it's enough just to take comfort in a job well done. Let's not forget that Van Gogh only sold one painting in his lifetime. I could only nod and smile years later when *Horrible Histories* arrived on our screens.

While I was busy working away on my side projects and putting less and less effort into the House of Fun – please don't sue this time, Suggs – I was called into the Scottish Television studio headquarters for a confab. Not many people realise that one of the side-effects of Wintergreen-derived salicylic acid (a staple in shampoos north of £75 a bottle) is paranoia. I can say that now but, at the time, I had a bad feeling about the meeting, which I put down to potential treachery from the production staff rather than chemicals seeping into my scalp. I was so paranoid I took to recording meetings using a tape recorder hidden in my briefcase. Here's an unedited extract from the conversation that afternoon:

> *Executive 1: Pat, there's really no need for you to leave your case on the table. Please could you just put it by your feet like everyone else?*
>
> *Pat: Don't worry about it. Anything you say clearly and enunciated to me, you can do so to the case.*
>
> *Executive 2: So, Pat, your contract runs out at the end of this series . . .*
>
> *Pat: Yeah, but enough about that. When are we going to start shooting the next series?*
>
> *Executive 1: Well, about that . . .*
>
> *Pat: Usually around mid-January, right?*
>
> *Executive 2: I think the point you might be missing . . .*
>
> *Pat: How about January 15th?*
>
> *Executive 1: Hmm.*
>
> *Pat: 16th?*
>
> *Executive 2: No, Pat.*

It went on like that for another ten minutes until the penny dropped by the time I reached late August. They fobbed me off with some nonsense about the show and my shtick having become tired, but I knew what was really going on. I've always been good at reading between the lines and I knew what they were saying. This was 1999 and our final episode was due to go out on 29 December. It didn't take a *How 2* presenter to work that one out. I'm sure you've all worked it out by now, so I just came out and said it: 'The show is ending because you're worried about the Millennium Bug, isn't that right? This is a Y2K issue, isn't it?'

'Um . . . er . . . yes . . .?'

In that hesitant, uncertain, stuttered reply, I had all the answer I needed. Of course, they couldn't have just come out and said it – that would have caused unnecessary alarm. It still makes me laugh to this day that the best cover story they could think of was to suggest that the show and my presenting of it were a tad stale.

It's a strange thing knowing something is coming to an end, whether it's a meal, a life or a beloved slice of Friday afternoon telly. You try and mentally prepare yourself for what's to come but, without the context, it doesn't really help. I always thought of it like footballers practising penalties in training – it's all well and good, but you can never replicate the atmosphere of a World Cup semi-final. More often than not in those last few weeks, my penalties were more England than Germany (i.e., rubbish, for those poor souls who aren't keen on sport).

As with the excellent meal/life analogy I used above, I had to get some things in order before the end. I didn't need to ask a waiter for the bill or organise funeral arrangements, but it was essential I thought about my next step. As has been mentioned previously, I was never a massive fan of the twins but, just as we were to cease working together after a decade, it seemed the ideal time to make an effort to get to know them a bit better. This process was made easier by the fact that a production assistant finally gave me a foolproof (or Patproof, as he referred to it) way of telling them apart. Apparently Martina always wore yellow and Melanie always wore red. Who knew? Apparently almost everybody.

I called the girls into my office and tried to break the news gently.

'Martina and Melanie, I've got some big news.'

'Yeah, we know . . . the show's ending,' they replied in unison.

It turned out they'd known for months, and had actually been informed even before I found out. But that was absolutely, definitely, unmistakably not something I obsessed about for months afterwards. My major concern was the enormous gaps in their CV. Ten years cheerleading on ITV might be useful for a job in the NFL, but this was England years before people over here started pretending they liked American football.

I needn't have worried. It transpired they'd been doing a business Masters at the University of Glasgow for years. There should be no plan B in showbusiness but it seemed they never really expected the show to last so they'd focused on the business. Once again, I was alone. Naturally. (Setting aside my wife and three wonderful children, who were married and born respectively in the period covered so far in this book.)

A farewell to childish things is never easy but I knew it was the right time, especially when I started receiving cease and desist letters from the producers of *Fun House*. I knew this would just be the start and that the show would be a mere footnote in my obituary. I mentioned *Seinfeld* at the start of this chapter but it was essential I didn't do a Jason Alexander and become exclusively associated with one TV programme. Or a Michael Richards, another of the programme's stars, who not only became exclusively associated with the same TV programme, but was also known for an uncontrolled, vicious, racist rant during a stand-up gig (he later apologised). No, if I was to emulate a *Seinfeld* actor, then it would have to be Julia Louis-Dreyfus – after all, I already had the phenomenal hair.

After the final day of filming, I hung around in the dressing room until everybody had left. I wanted to have some time to myself to say goodbye to the old girl. By the old girl, I mean the Fun House. One of the production staff gave me a key to lock up and I took a deep breath and walked back into what some (I) refer to as the greatest colosseum of them all. The one in Rome is nowhere near multicoloured enough for my taste.

I broke through the wall at the house's entrance. It felt like an aggressive act, even though I did it with the tenderness she deserved. Once I crossed the threshold, the act of destruction felt right. It was a fitting metaphor for the show – everything that we build up eventually gets torn down.

I made my way to the balloon run, as so many children had done before me. At that time there were no balloons in it, which again felt so fitting – where once there was joy, now there was emptiness.

From there I went over to the giant steps. Not the most spectacular of the obstacles but by no means a pushover. Leading to many of the other house features, kids would normally have to scale it a few times and it could really become gruelling as fatigue sets in. It was our travelator from *Gladiators*, but with a more pleasing subtlety. As I clambered up, I was reminded that we designed it without jeans as tight as mine in mind.

I walked past the Small Step for Mankind. I've never really liked it or understood it, so I didn't really engage.

The A-Frame was a completely different prospect. So simple, so effective, so iconic. As I clambered over, it felt like the perfect metaphor – you work hard to climb up but then you have to come down.

The climbing net really isn't that big when you're a fully grown adult but that doesn't make it a piece of cake. There's a reason that we don't make ladders out of fabric – it's so much harder to climb without the structural integrity of wood or metal. As I swayed and struggled to find my footing, I couldn't help but be reminded of my attempts to keep the show on the air – desperately trying to climb but finding little to no support beneath me.

The Snake in the Box was much like the balloon run, and the show. It had once held so much excitement and potential but right now was barren and empty.

I took hold of the handles on the flying fox and pulled my knees to my chest. Gravity very slowly transported me from stage top left of the house to stage top right. As I slowly creaked along, I looked up at the supporting structure. Had it really been five years since I'd first seen those stress fractures in the supporting beams? Time really does wait for no man.

As I walked over to the Sunken Well, I was reminded of my initial reservations about the obstacle. I had no problem with it in and of itself, but the name was a nonsense. This was one of the highest points of the Fun House, so what kind of idiot would build a well there? Obviously, you put a well at ground level for reasons of efficiency. I was strongly against this kind of flawed internal logic and, while those feelings were still there, I was also aware that it didn't matter any more (I wasn't to know that Challenge TV would later become a thing).

I grabbed the Fireman's Pole and grimaced as the rust marks pulled at my skin just as it had pulled at the skin of so many children before me. At the bottom, I looked at the broken skin and thought about how it would heal. Time heals all wounds, so they say, but I just didn't believe that about one particular wound that burned deep inside me.

I made for the ball run and tried to pick my knees up. It was advice that I gave every single child that entered the House, but scant few listened. Like so many things, it felt like hard work to trudge through but, once I got to the other side, I looked back and was so very sad it was over.

I sat at the top of the Wild Slide with my feet dangling down it, my feet resting closer to the bottom of the slide than the top. I thought about the downwards trajectory of all things and how one can never go back. Although, in this case, I could easily have gone back – the friction on the slide means it would be very easy to climb up and, to get myself down, I had to shimmy myself in a very undignified manner.

I climbed back up the Giant Steps with an aching in my thighs. I had wanted to do a perfect circuit of the House but there's no way to do that. I always thought it was a design flaw but I suppose because the kids would tag in and out, you don't want to create the temptation for them to simply do a lap round the whole thing.

I made for the Danger Nets and, as I dragged myself along them, I was struck by how meaningless everything is. Things are just what we decide they are. These nets weren't dangerous; they were annoying to climb across and not very exciting as a spectator sport. We called them dangerous to pretend there was something interesting about them. They were in no way dangerous. In fact, they were probably one of the safest things as those ropes were one of the few things in the House that weren't flammable.

I took myself down the Bobsleigh, although the confetti canon wasn't rigged so there was no way to mask how unimpressive it actually is. We only got the budget for it because I had been confident of forming a *Cool Runnings* tie-in but that never came to fruition due to a number of reasons.

I climbed to the top of the Tall Tower and was reminded that it wasn't even the highest point of the Fun House. Just another reminder that sometimes the heights we feel we've reached aren't all that we think they are.

I made my way to the Crawl Tube and struggled to wriggle my way through. It wasn't only the commissionability of *Fun House* that had aged badly in the last ten years. No longer did I have the slender waist of a 12-year-old; I had let my 38-year-old body go to the extent that I had the 28in waist of a 17-year-old.

I had to go down the pole again for the same reason I had to do the steps twice. This time it was a bit less annoying, though, because the pole is more fun than the steps, even with the rust.

With every obstacle conquered, I lay in the foam blocks near the exit. I couldn't bring myself to leave, so I slipped into a deep yet restless sleep thinking about how loss is one of the few things to be experienced by all sentient beings.

One of the great joys of my life has been people coming up to me and telling me they associate the show (and by extension, me) with the feeling of getting home on a Friday and knowing there was no need to do any homework. Is there any better feeling than that of being a child without responsibilities? Even as my weekends grow dimmer, I will always know that for entire generations of children my presence meant no less than the start of the weekend. When that Friday comes and I'm not there to see it, and the first line of my Wikipedia page moves from the present to the past tense, I know it's *Fun House* I'll be remembered for and I couldn't be prouder.

When the final episode aired after what seemed like an eternity, it felt only right to arrange a viewing party at our place. After lengthy negotiations with the missus and her finally acquiescing to recording *Neighbours*, we were good to go. The red and yellow invitations were a thing of beauty and I arranged a string quartet to play the theme tune on a loop in our living room for an hour prior to the show starting. I'm not ashamed to admit there were a few tears that afternoon but that could be because my wife insisted I cater the thing myself and chopping onions has always had that effect on me. Obviously, a weekday afternoon isn't the best time for a party, but my nearest and dearest all made an appearance. As the closing credits rolled for the 146th and final time and I looked into the eyes of those most important to me – my wife, my kids, Dave Benson Phillips – I knew the six of us in that room had shared something very special that day. But now, it was time for a new chapter . . . so it probably makes sense to end this one.

Chapter 15

Daphne and Celeste – 'Ooh Stick You!'

They don't ask just anyone to open for Jay-Z at Glastonbury and I was so thrilled for the girls when they got the chance. Neil Buchanan used to sing this down the phone at me as a prank call, not realising that I had paid to get Caller ID. I never told him.

I was in quite a sombre mood at the end of that party. Most people didn't hang around for long afterwards. I think they could sense that I needed some time to process this and get my head together. I've always surrounded myself with sensitive and emotionally intelligent people and they were able to sense that it was time to go. As I rolled around on the floor wailing and pounding my fists, I noticed that Dave was the exception and was still hanging around.

'What shall we watch now, Pat?' he asked with a big grin.

I don't remember what we watched but I do remember that Dave ate all of the crisps. *All* of the crisps. We had really over-bought on them but he just kept on going.

The next day, I went for a walk along the South Bank. It was one of those cold, crisp days with a fair breeze, which struggled to make it through the dense layers of mousse and hairspray in my hair so walking was quite an effort with my barnet producing a sizeable amount of wind resistance. I was pleased to get beyond the Royal Festival Hall and just before the book stall to that bit where there are always skateboarders. There were about six of them doing some pretty impressive tricks. I watched them for a while and, on a couple of occasions, applauded a particularly well executed fakie kick flip or 360 nose grab. They didn't seem to notice that I was there.

I walked a bit further and the cold began to creep through my denim jacket into my bones. I didn't really feel like having a coffee but decided to get one all the same. As I entered the Tate Modern, I was thinking about those skateboarders. There was one older guy, which was a bit weird, but the rest were smack in the middle of the *Fun House* demographic. They should have been watching the night before. I couldn't decide what made me feel sadder – the fact that they didn't acknowledge me or the fact that I had clearly been standing there, going as far as to applaud and shout, 'Look, it's me!' in the hope that they would acknowledge me.

'Thank you.'

Those words took me away from ten minutes ago and snapped me back into the present. I looked to see where the words had come from. They had come from a round face with green eyes and a little pink bobble hat. It was the briefest of exchanges but it meant so much. I was beginning to realise why I had gone for that walk and what I needed but, in that moment, when it was actually given to me, it was blindingly obvious. That was why I went for a walk. That was why I was wearing the brightly coloured tie-dye clothes with the words 'Fun House' in big, bold letters at the centre. And that was why I was trying to make eye contact with everyone I passed. That was why I spent so long waiting for the skateboarders to see me. I was in mourning and I wanted somebody to mourn with me. The nation had suffered a huge loss and I just wanted somebody to share that loss with me. I couldn't take the burden of this tragedy alone and even the smallest gesture to say 'we're in this together' somehow made the whole thing more manageable.

I doubt she'll ever know what she did for me that morning. In that briefest of exchanges when I held open the door, she walked through it and on the way said, 'Thank you,' she hugged my soul, took it by the hand and said, 'It's not just you.' Words have such power, which is probably why poems can be really good even when they're short (especially in the case of limericks). What she said was 'thank you' but what she really said was, 'I (and everybody else) appreciate the 146 slices of joy that you gave us. There were countless prizes given out to contestants but the real prizes were the million moments of pure bliss that you brought to the world. We are all guilty of taking it for granted but, now that the dark day has come, I just want to say thank you. I will always be thankful.'

I felt so warmed that I didn't even need the coffee. The other thing that lifted my spirits was a text message that arrived almost as soon as I stepped back out into the cold. I was so touched by it that I made the decision to keep it on my phone. It meant making a difficult decision as to which of the ten messages already stored would make way, but when I tell you the backstory, you'll understand.

It was from Neil Buchanan. We were both apples in the eye of ITV and were frequently referred to as lynchpins of the children's schedule. We were like brothers – we hated each other. We bickered and squabbled constantly whenever we were in the same room and would never choose to socialise. So when I received a text reading: 'fancy dinner m8? Rly enjoyed the last show . . .' I was touched. In my current state, this was the most beautiful combination of words and abbreviations any man could hope to receive.

'Hello, mate!' I said breezily when Neil walked into the bar at the restaurant.

'You're paying by the way.'

I laughed, but Neil was serious. He cast his eyes to the very bottom of the wine list so fast I was worried he'd get whiplash.

We had a table by the window and Neil chatted away happily about his day. We'd known each other a very long time so I suppose it wasn't unusual that there would be a familiarity between us but we had never talked this way before. I don't remember where we first met, but there was a day when we went on a teambuilding trip that sums up our relationship pretty well.

The suits upstairs thought that we should go paintballing because that was fashionable at the time. The place they booked was in Surrey, which they had erroneously assumed was on the District Line somewhere. After an almighty kerfuffle, we were able to sort out five cars to drive down. Our car consisted of Dave Benson Phillips (driving), Fern Britton (navigating), Trevor McDonald (patiently sitting between me and Neil Buchanan), Neil Buchanan (sitting on Trevor McDonald's left) and me (sitting two seats over from Neil Buchanan and staring out of the window like a beautiful golden retriever on a summer's day).

'Next stop, Task Force!' announced Dave through a mouthful of crisps. Fern was in charge of the radio as well as the map and did an excellent job cycling through the stations so that each song was slightly more up tempo than the last. I recommend that approach – it really creates a growing sense of anticipation and energy.

He will deny this to his dying breath, but Neil pinched my leg first. He leaned across Sir Trevor (née Trevor) and got me on the right calf. I was wearing denim cut-offs so he was able to take a couple of hairs with him. He benefited from the element of surprise, so even though it was a clumsy effort, it hit home. I bided my time. I could sense him squirming out of the corner of my eye and enjoyed the fact that he was on edge. He knew it was coming but didn't know when. A couple of times he made a slight movement as if he were going to go in for a second attack, but we both know that would have been suicide. To go in for two unprovoked attacks would have made me a martyr and him an out-of-control, unprovoked aggressor.

The bend was ever so slight but I took my chance with aplomb. The centrifugal force only slightly arced my body into Trevor's, but the tight packing of our legs meant that Neil was helpless to move. My right hand snapped like a viper. I've always been good at finding that point just above the knee cap that is really painful even when it's not pressed that hard. He nearly hit the roof.

'Pat!' Fern spun round and glared at me. Trevor said nothing but I could feel his disappointed gaze on my left cheek. Dave was wiping his fingers on his trousers and looking for something in the glove box. I still think it's unfair that I was the one admonished just because I had landed the better blow, but there we are. To be fair, the chastising was shared equally among the two of us as we continued to act up for the rest of the journey.

Still, it was his fault, he started it. I don't know why Fern always got to sit in the front either, so unfair.

'So help me I'll turn this car around,' threatened Dave after I reacted to Neil extracting another couple of leg hairs.

'You actually need to. This is a dead end . . . I'm sorry,' said Fern as Neil sniggered.

We kept pinching and slapping. Trevor's glasses were dislodged no fewer than three times as we flailed our limbs in the direction of the other. We then resorted to name-calling.

'More like *Fart Attack*,' I said in response to Neil's, 'With you as host, were they not tempted to call it *Bum House*?'

Obviously, we questioned each other's hygiene in increasingly witless ways: 'Can we open a window? I'm struggling to breathe because of how bad Neil stinks.' The Oscar Wilde brothers we were not.

'I didn't know we were going past a sewage works. Oh no, wait. It's just Pat . . .' And so on. We also got in frequent digs about each other's professional careers.

'I think it's good you don't do *Top of the Pops* too often. It's easy to become overexposed.'

'True. I think the only better thing to do would be to never be asked to present it ever.'

'It was a good move to have four kids on each show because they can always be there to provide some charisma to make up for your lack of it.'

'I love that you're able to be so comfortable doing something as boring as drawing. I mean you could just do the big *Art Attack* thing that looks good from the sky because that's the only bit people like but you have the courage to do loads of bullshit before that.'

We kept it up the whole journey until Trevor screamed. The man can hit a surprisingly high note. So can Neil, who yelped as I delivered an expert wet willy around the back of Trevor's head. That gave me the last laugh as we got out of the car but Neil definitely had the next.

'Head over to the safe area where you'll get your goggles and helmets,' said the pimply youth who would be the one sending us off into the battlefield. I knew Neil wanted me to look at him. I could feel him pleading with me to look his way and, stupidly, I gave him the satisfaction. I caught his gaze and he pointed, 'Enjoy your helmet hair, Cowpat Sharp,' he cackled before he threw his head back, danced a little jig and screamed, 'Aaaaah!' in a manner that made it sound like he was exploding. At that moment, I could but wish.

I put on the goggles and the helmet. I'm still not really ready to talk about it, but I think I've told you enough of this story to showcase the typical interactions between Neil and me. I'll give you some highlights, though. I can tell you that Neil and I were on the same team but didn't contribute much because at the start of each game we would shoot each other immediately and then bicker incessantly on the sidelines. I can tell you that Eamonn Holmes is deceptively agile and an excellent shot. I can tell you that Anne Diamond is fiercely competitive to the point where she is willing to wipe paint off her arm when the stewards aren't looking. She also holds no loyalty to *This Morning* partner Nick Owen in the heat of battle.

I can also tell you that there was a tense moment when a junior member of one of the teams was adjusting his goggles and got hit on the shoulder. 'You could have had my eye out!' said the aspiring children's television writer from the north-east whose name I forget. Luckily, a paint pellet wasn't fired into his eye but a certain glint was.

Neil would also call into my radio shows and try to get through the producers so that he could swear on air. I, in turn, would go and sabotage his giant Art Attacks. He had the benefit of editing so those pictures of his face with stink lines or pithy rhymes making fun of his penis never made it to air. I was live and therefore more vulnerable, but I'm happy to say that for all of his efforts, my superb production teams ensured that he only ever got one 'wassock' on to the air.

It wasn't until Neil's tailor-made order of lobster stuffed with another lobster with a gold leaf and truffle sauce arrived that conversation turned to *Fun House*. Even at that point, I hadn't twigged his real motive for this meal.

'So, end of an era old boy!' he said, while holding his knife as though it was a pen like an idiot. 'As I was watching, a huge grin spread over my face,' he said, trying to break into a lobster claw like a two-year old trying to do a Rubik's cube. 'I thought to myself – this tripe is finally ending!' he finished with a cackle. He just wanted to gloat. I should have seen it coming. 'So what will you do now? Maybe you could be a stand-in for a pile of manure. You've got the look and the smell down to a T. Failing that, maybe you could get a job shouting at children in a play-ground while they play games and making terrible jokes to people around you who aren't listening.'

It was a long meal. I can at least look back with satisfaction that he had no idea that Challenge TV would emerge and give *Fun House* an even more regular platform than it had had in its heyday. It's so lovely to think that now every day is like a Friday.

Sadly, these kinds of rivalries aren't uncommon in the world of celebrity and showbusiness. I already told you about the Damon Albarn–Liam Gallagher spat and these sorts of things were all over the place. Andi Peters and Timmy Mallet; Pato Banton and Mr Motivator; Mr Bronson from *Grange Hill* and Floella Benjamin; Emma Forbes and the guy who played Mr Blobby; Mystic Meg and pretty much everyone. The list goes on and on but, in a time before Twitter, a lot of these spats were able to remain behind closed doors.

Some of them were just because people rubbed each other up the wrong way. Others might be because of an ill-fated relationship, but quite often it was professional jealousy. It's quite a small world and people are aware once they reach a certain age that it may not last for ever. Personally, I would never begrudge success and even in the jobs I missed out on (like *Countdown*) I was still able to enjoy and respect the artist in question. I'm sad to say that I was in the minority in this view and, in one instance, the frustration of a career not going to plan was directed at me.

I would only discover years later that an unnamed presenter had built up enormous resentment towards me and it did explain a few things. He was a massive fan of *Fun House* (weren't we all?) and just after he broke into kids' TV in 1992, he set his heart on taking over the show. He had grown up listening to me on the radio and was inspired not just to be like me, but to *be* me.

We first met at one of Jeremy Bates' parties. Unnamed Presenter came up and told me he'd been listening to me for years. There was a very noticeable gap in which he didn't follow that up with a compliment. Instead, he stared at my hair and slowly licked his lips. I told him it was nice to meet him and made for the kitchen where I could see that the SodaStream had become free. He blocked my path.

'So are you going to keep doing *Fun House?*'

I looked at him for a minute trying to read what type of joke this was. I couldn't get it so I just shrugged my shoulders and said, 'Of course.'

He grabbed my wrist and moved his gaze from my hair down to my eyes. 'I'd like to host it,' he said, tightening his grip.

I laughed. 'And we'd all like to have a million pounds and be married to Pamela Anderson!' I said, and whoever was nearby laughed uproariously. Unnamed Presenter let go and I thought no more of it.

He would come to recordings from time to time and I just thought he was a fan. Quite often, we'd eat together when I would be sitting at my regular table in Tito's and I'd see him peering through the window and invite him in. We would eat in silence but I still had a nice time.

Some strange things would happen occasionally and it's only in retrospect that I've realised they were the occasions when Unnamed Presenter was around. I would always know when he was there because he would sit himself in the middle of the front row. He had excellent posture and would sit there, barely moving an inch for the entire recording. Such was his love for the show that he wouldn't even break his focus by clapping or even smiling.

Every now and then the apples we had in the green room would taste a bit like raw chicken. It took me a while to realise what the slightly unusual tang was, but I only figured it out when I had salmonella that time. In between bouts of vomiting, I looked up to see Unnamed Presenter talking to the producer. He had a big flipchart with him and was making a presentation entitled 'Fun House with Unnamed Presenter'. I admired his resourcefulness and dedication to the show that he was so keen to find a way to make it work without me for the sake of the fans in the event of my death. Obviously, it wouldn't have worked but I have a lot of time for a 'can-do' attitude. The next time he was in Scotland for a recording, we had one of our impromptu dinners and he had a Tesco carrier bag. I kicked it over when going to the toilet and a whole bunch of chicken breasts fell out. He looked a bit flustered and said that they were cheaper and leaner in Scotland so he always got them there. I bought all of my chicken in Glasgow for the next six years, which I now realise was stupid.

In later years, we would both be working at London's Heart. I tended to have better slots than Unnamed Presenter and, although there were never any chickeny apples, I would occasionally find myself locked in the toilet and experience an exchange along these lines:

Unnamed Presenter: Oh, hi there, Matt [Producer].

Matt: Hi, Unnamed Presenter. Have you seen Pat? His show starts in ten.

Unnamed Presenter: No, I've not.

Pat: Hi, Matt, I'm in the cubicle.

Matt: Why are you in there?

Pat: I find that my links are at their most peppy when I have empty bowels.

Matt: Well, you're cutting it fine.

Pat: I've been done for minutes but the door is stuck.

Unnamed Presenter: Yeah, I don't know what that's about. I've been trying to get him out.

Matt: It looks like it's been screwed shut. Again. Didn't this happen last week?

Unnamed Presenter: Yeah, it's really weird. Hey, Matt, while you're here, I've updated my presentation about me hosting Drive Time.

Matt: Not now, Unnamed Presenter.

Unnamed Presenter: Look, this stuff is good to go. If we can't get those 4in lag bolts out of the door, which will take a while without the right spanner, then I could just jump straight in.

Matt: That won't be necessary. Aren't you off today?

Unnamed Presenter: Yeah, but I was around so thought I'd drop in. By the looks of it, may be lucky that I did!

Matt: I'll get maintenance. Pat, drop the Wheatus tickets competition into the third link, OK?

Pat: Sure thing, boss.

It would normally transpire that Unnamed Presenter would have the correct spanner and be able to release me just in time. 'You never know when you might need one,' was what he told me. I would carry an adjustable spanner around with me for years after that, but that again feels like a mistake.

With *Fun House* no more, you could be forgiven for thinking that I would have fallen back on my hair (and not just because it had so much volume and body that it would make a highly serviceable crash mat). It seems strange that a man so renowned for his 'do didn't ever make that much money directly from it. At the time, I didn't think about it that much. I was a presenter and the hair helped me to present at near superhuman levels. I was, of course, aware of shampoo adverts but there was only one occasion when I seriously pursued it or thought that it would happen.

I've always liked L'Oréal. I like that they went for that name instead of the more tedious English name of 'The Oreal', and I think it does an excellent job of taking a real high-end shampoo that can do a job at professional level and making it accessible for the high street. As a keen Arsenal fan, I obviously had feelings about David Ginola who was playing for bitter rivals Tottenham Hotspur at the time.

I knew he was handy at set pieces, had flair in abundance and wasn't averse to whipping off his shirt to answer any body-shaming critics. What I didn't know was that he was my main rival for a lucrative advertising campaign. I figured they must have been in talks with other people and I was trying to work out who was in the same league as me hair-wise. There obviously aren't many, so I was able to narrow it down and Ginola was on the list. So, too, were Mick Hucknall and Jennifer Aniston.

I found out it was down to me or Dave about a week before they were making their decision. Coincidentally, the Arsenal were playing Spurs that weekend and I had tickets to go along and watch. I think the game ended 1–1 but the only point of note was when José Dominguez got away down the left and put in a deep cross. Ginola stooped at the far post to plant a header in and I nearly got punched for cheering. I couldn't help it, though – it was a wet day and he took the sodden, muddy ball right to the fringe. I thought it was suicide to do that so close to decision time.

Later that week, I was invited to a Hewlett-Packard event and I knew Dave would be there as they were the main shirt sponsor of Spurs. I was intrigued to see what I would be like with the two of us in the same room with a lucrative contract hanging overhead. The answer was 'absolutely fine'. We didn't speak and Dave didn't even seem to know who I was.

My agent broke the news to me and I watched a lot of TV over the coming weeks waiting to see his finished product. Then one day it happened, during the break in *Emmerdale*. His hair looked exquisite and I involuntarily stood and applauded in my living room.

I was a little disappointed, though. I'd made an extravagant pitch about using L'Oréal to get the gunge out of my hair at the end of a day's filming. In the end, the quality of the hair spoke for itself, but I think we really could have done something special with a narrative as strong as that.

If advertisers and television executives couldn't see the value of what I had to offer then, not for the first time, I would have to make my own opportunities. I never had the benefit of a university education, but I'll hazard I've spent more time around campuses than almost anyone (excluding lecturers). Why? That's a whole other story (or chapter).

Chapter 16

Bon Jovi – 'Livin' on a Prayer'

Such a beautiful song. For me, it has that rare quality of evoking two distinct times – the '80s and the university scene of the early '00s where it was ubiquitous. How can you not love this song? The lyrics say it all: 'We've got each other and something, something . . . love. We'll give it a shot. Woah, something, something . . . whoa, whoa . . . living on a prayer.'

The period immediately after *Fun House* was a strange one. It was important that I took stock of my life and realised how lucky I'd been and tried to work out exactly what I wanted to do going forward. The greats always know exactly when to call it a day and I didn't want to outstay my welcome like some fading heavyweight making a series of ill-advised comebacks purely for the money. I wanted to be like a 1990s French footballer who wasn't Ginola – aka Eric Cantona – walking out as a young man at the top of my game, not like Neil Buchanan desperately clinging on in spite of my advancing years. Admittedly, the decision to stop making the show hadn't been mine, but who's to say I wouldn't have packed it in before too long anyway? (Me, in a series of begging letters sent to the powers-that-be in the months following the decision, in which I literally wrote the words: 'Please look into your hearts – I would gladly do this show well into my 80s if you'd only let me.')

I needed to take a long, hard look in the mirror but that wasn't an issue since it was always a pleasure and never a chore. Who was I? What was my particular set of skills? Unlike Liam Neeson in *Taken*, I am better at segues into competitions than I am hunting down and killing the sex-traffickers responsible for kidnapping my teenage daughter. My own daughter's godparents once took her to a county fête and I was meant to meet them there. I was given very clear instructions as to their location and I still couldn't find them. No. After a profound period of soul-searching and intense discussions with a variety of therapists, I knew exactly who I was and how to proceed with my life. I knew my limitations and my strengths. I knew what I had to do next.

The audition for *Newsnight* did not go well. The BBC, in their wisdom, were good enough to let me do a trial run. After the difficulties I'd encountered with the *Fun House* pilot, I left nothing to chance when it came to the flagship current affairs show. All TV is basically the same – it's about making a connection with people. From Gore Vidal to Kim Kardashian, all any of us want is to be heard and to feel as though people like what they're hearing. Plus, as Gore, Kim or myself will tell you, being rich, famous and sexy is, unlike ham and pineapple, a pretty great combo.

John Prescott was kind enough to let me rope him in for the audition tape. 'Two Jags' has always had a lot of time for me since I'd stayed behind with him for hours after the 1998 Brit Awards and used my industrial-strength hair dryer to remedy the damage done by Chumbawamba and that bucket of ice-cold water. That whole thing was a huge misunderstanding anyway, the papers suggesting it was to do with the Liverpool dock workers and their industrial dispute, but I bumped into the lads not long ago and they were adamant this was simply their own attempt to get the Ice Bucket Challenge off the ground. Either way, as I slowly warmed every nook and cranny of the Deputy Prime Minister's body, I mentally made a note to call in a favour further down the line.

How would I fare without identical twins or a go-kart track? Would I ask Johnny P what his favourite subject at school was? Would I accuse him of looking too clean and push a gunge-filled pie in his face? I opened with something light and asked about the benefits of the Kyoto Treaty but, I'm sorry to say, Johnny simply didn't have the charisma for live TV. I motioned with my hands in a manner that implored him to up the energy, but he just kept droning on about the need to reduce greenhouse gas emissions. When my trademark waving of the arms failed to cut it with Tony Blair's deputy, I knew I was in trouble. Things went from bad to Buchanan when I asked him his favourite ice-cream flavour.

I write all this, of course, with the benefit of hindsight. At the time, I took John's stern glares as a sign that he was giving the question serious consideration. When the producer calmly stated, 'We've seen enough,' it seemed to me quite clear that I had the job in the bag. That's one of the very few drawbacks of being an optimist. Another is that I was so sure I'd get the job that I had nothing else planned. Plus I'd put down a deposit on a house. If ever I needed some irons in the fire, it was that twenty-year stretch from the year 2000 to the present day.

That winter, I spent many an hour sitting in my office-cum-toilet trying to decipher what made my fans tick. I'd presented a beloved show for a decade and all I needed to do was work out what united my fanbase. And then it hit me like a bucket of gunge to the face – school.

Yes, there was the odd cougar who tuned in to *Fun House* purely for a sight of my magnificent buttocks, but the bulk of the viewers were children and associated the programme with coming home from school. Given that the show started in 1989, a fair few of these kids would no longer be kids and they might even have left school. Using a calculator, an exercise book and a substantial chunk of my free time, I eventually deduced that some of them might even be in their 20s by now.

I've often thought that one of the reasons people have so much fondness for *Fun House* is the association with Friday afternoons. We were very lucky to have the slot immediately after the school week ends, that moment when the clock hits four and the satchel hits floor. There is that electric feeling of freedom and excitement that comes from school being over and the grim, mood-crushing *Antiques Roadshow* on Sunday evening seeming like a speck on the horizon. The *Fun House* theme tune is Pavlov's bell.

I'd heard a bit about 'Back 2 School' disco nights from Andi Peters but they struck me as vaguely absurd. From what I could gather, revellers were encouraged to wear uniforms and the music played was the stuff they might associate with their schooldays. That was it. I liked the idea that uniforms could be sexier than regulation, and planned the tight-trouser, six-buttons-undone combo that I would go for, but other than that the evenings sounded faintly ridiculous and the school aspect appeared to be a total misnomer. Fortunately, necessity is the mother of invention, so you can call me Mummy Sharp.

That's a metaphor – please don't, I'd find it really uncomfortable.

I devised a club night built around the actual feeling of being at school. It would finally put the 'Back to School' into Back 2 School and the disco aspect would feel earned at the end of the evening. The first event took place at Jesters in Southampton and everything was planned to the last detail. Clubbers would arrive at 8.40am, register would be taken and then it was time for prayers and morning assembly. Double maths followed by Chemistry next, then morning break, English, History then Chemistry before lunch and finally PE. Obviously, no alcohol was to be consumed during this seven-hour stretch and chewing gum was prohibited. The investors said I was being too rigid but they didn't realise that the school disco can only really work if the punters feel like they've been at school. That release is absolute vital and the four people who made it through the entire day would doubtless agree with me.

It's funny how life works. One minute you're the pigeon, the next you're the statue. I was walking through the grim streets of Portswood, Southampton, that night feeling at my lowest ebb. No amount of conditioner was going to improve my mood because I'd given it my all and still failed. People didn't want eight periods of academic discipline leading up to a spot of dancing and I just couldn't understand why. I trudged along the pavement with my hands in my pockets and my head hanging downwards like some kind of hirsute Charlie Brown. And then I heard it. The most beautiful sound in the galaxy. If music be the food of love, play on . . .

It was the opening bars of the theme tune to *Fun House* emanating from a club not 15ft away. The music had me under its spell and I followed the tune like a man in a trance. I opened the door of this golden palace and was greeted by a sign declaring the night to deliver '100 per cent absolute solid cheese shite guaranteed'. Finally, I had found my people.

Like a moth inexplicably drawn to a flame, I made my way towards the stage area, strode up the stairs and stood next to the resident DJ. The crowd went wild. They hadn't heard this song and been confronted with His Patness simultaneously since they were kids watching telly. It was – obviously, setting aside my wedding day and the births of my children – the most perfect moment of my entire life. So perfect, in fact, that Martine McCutcheon could have been singing about it in her smashing song (she wasn't, she once told me in Soho House, it was about the time she found an ideal parking space in central London and reversed into it first time with ease). When the whooping and hollering had subsided, the DJ even let me introduce a few drinking games and tell the odd joke. Or, as I like to think if it – I came, I saw, I compèred.

JK Rowling has often spoken about the fact that Harry Potter came to her fully formed on a train journey from Manchester to London. I know that feeling exactly because it was similar for me during that fateful night on the South Coast. I can recall standing in front of the audience and concocting the notion of 'Student Nights'; that is to say, nights aimed at students.

Over time, I began to develop an act. Like Dean Martin in his prime, I wanted to demonstrate the fact that I am nothing if not a Renaissance man. I mastered an array of magic tricks, learned to tap dance, honed a series of devastatingly accurate impressions, nailed a stand-up comedy routine and memorised large chunks of Shakespeare's greatest soliloquies. Over time, with the encouragement of bar owners up and down the land, I refined the act further and further until it was at its tightest and purest and all I was doing was waving.

Ideas started to come thick and fast, like school porridge on a Japanese bullet train. One that I was delighted with was the notion of recreating *Fun House* for all those unlucky enough to have been unable to make it on to the show during the ITV run. The posters had my face and the words 'Fun House' in enormous letters, so it was perfectly reasonable to assume the masses would expect a little more than just waving.

In a flurry of activity, I visited venues up and down the country and took measurements to be sure we could effectively recreate the magic of Friday afternoon telly in a series of crappy dives. I spoke to my ball pond guy (shout-out to Jeremy!) and had a fairly good stab at installing race tracks in venues that would allow it. How would I do it? Could we pull this off? What was I going to tell my wife about the amount of money I was pumping into this?

I rocked up at the first official *Fun House* night to be informed that there had been a slight rejig and that instead of £34,000-worth of *Fun House* reconstructions, students would be having races to see who could down a Snakebite the quickest while the theme tune played. I think that's every bit as good as my own suggestions and it works really well.

I love those student gigs and feel as though I can connect directly with the fans in a way that isn't always possible through a camera lens. The fact is that you get bigger crowds at Roehampton uni than we ever did in the Glasgow studio. You might even say I'm doing better now than I was in the '90s. You might, but it would be, at best, barely credible.

One major change from the '90s was atop my head. I came to a decision that made headlines around this point and decided to mull it over and the result was mullet over. I knew I was a Samson figure and that much of my power came from my hair, but I had to make a change and draw a line in the sand. Finally, I was making peace with the fact that *Fun House* was over and it wasn't coming back. I needed to do something to mark that, something that couldn't be undone.

I hadn't really believed in the concept of a soul before – the idea that there is a spiritual or mystical part of you that is the true essence of who you are – but as I began seriously to contemplate the unthinkable, I wondered if my hair was my soul. They say that the eyes are the gateway to the soul, and that's often the bit of you that people stare lovingly into; but for me, in the most tender moments, people have always stared into my hair. It stands to reason that my hair is the window to my soul, so what would I be without it?

I dipped into the philosophy section of my library but, after a while, just looked for some famous quotations on the Internet. Saint Augustine said that 'Love is the beauty of the soul'. In destroying the mullet, would I be destroying love? It seemed likely. CS Lewis said, 'You don't have a soul. You are a soul. You have a body.' Was I my hair? If I destroyed it, would I destroy myself? Where did the hair end and I begin? (At the root I guess). I kept reading and came across a quotation from Fatboy Slim: 'Right about now. The funk soul brother. Check it out now. The funk soul brother.' I didn't really know what that meant but, for some reason, it really steeled my resolve and I decided that I would do it. I would take the risk. Maybe it was because the Fatboy had very short hair but still got to be married to Zoe Ball for a bit.

I cried less than I thought I would both during and after the cut. I would say, all in all, that it took about sixteen hours, pretty much the same as a fairly long labour for a new mum, but far more painful. I couldn't tell you how long the malaise lasted. I feel like I wandered around in a fog for anywhere between a day and seven years. Sometimes, I felt quite good about it. In some ways (for example, literally) it was like a weight had been lifted from my shoulders. At other times, I'd catch a glimpse of myself in the reflection of a car or a shop window and almost be physically sick when I realised what I'd lost.

Sometimes, I'd be excited and feel invigorated by the challenge of life without the mullet. Had I been riding its coat-tails this whole time? Was this the chance to reinvent myself and prove that I was more than a man with wonderful, wonderful hair? Inevitably, these thoughts would be punctured by doubt and I'd plunge into a well of despair. What had I done? Could God ever forgive me for interfering with one of his greatest creations?

After weeks of struggling to recognise my reflection and suffering from an acute case of cold neck, I accepted my fate. It sounds silly but, when I noticed after three months that I hadn't died, I realised that my life wasn't over.

I was older and the kids who were my fans were older. These teenagers didn't want Fun House Pat; they wanted Lewd Story Pat, Provocative Gesture Pat, Quadruple Sugared-Tea Pat. Fortunately, there is a Pat for all seasons and I love nothing more than giving the people what they want. These weren't excitable primary school children I was dealing with any more; these were tomorrow's leaders, those bastions of good behaviour and moral fortitude – university students.

We are all of us guilty of upward and downward conversions. That is to say, if I'm talking to a builder then I might drop an 'H' or two and liberally sprinkle in words like 'mate' and 'pal'. If and when I am honoured by the Queen, I'll more than likely use the kind of posh voice my mum adopted whenever she was on the phone. That's just the nature of human beings and there's nothing wrong with it at all. It's the same story at those student nights.

The first three times I was asked if I'd engaged in sexual relations with the twins by drunken teenagers, I ignored it. The fourth time, I shrugged. By the twentieth time, I had concocted the kind of erotic fiction that would put EL James in the shade. Maybe even 50 of them.

I felt awful because my relationship with the twins had never been anything but professional. My intense desire to give people what they want had resulted in a tale of extreme raunchiness set in a disused go-kart. I need to make things right and knew exactly what to do. I'd 'retcon' it.

For those who've had sex and might not know the term, 'retcon' is a portmanteau word that combines retroactive and continuity. It basically refers to the practice in films like *Star Wars* to add a piece of new information that imposes a different interpretation on previously described events, typically used to facilitate a dramatic plot shift or account for an inconsistency. Essentially, it is a way of reassuring nerds that George Lucas had every single minuscule detail mapped out since he came up with the first film in the 1970s.

Obviously, it was too late for me to say I hadn't slept with the twins since I was boasting about it five times a night in clubs the length and breadth of this fair land. The only obvious solution at this point was to actually do the deed so I didn't feel so guilty about lying to my fanbase. The first thing I did was to float the idea with my wife and she was so understanding that it almost seemed like sarcasm. Her exact words were, 'Well, you can certainly ask them.'

I dialled the girls almost paralysed with fear as my wife stood beside me with hands on hips. At least they lived together and I'd only have to go through this terrible ordeal once. I wrote their names on my palm in biro so as to make as good an impression as possible. They answered in unison and I took the plunge:

'Martina, Melanie . . . I hope all's well. I know it's been a while but I was just wondering if you'd be interested in a threesome at some point soon . . .?'

They declined. Perhaps I should have kept things classy and referred to it as a *ménage à trois*, but it's so often after the event that one thinks of the perfect thing to say. I couldn't let my fans down now so the only thing for it was to continue to claim I'd 'banged' the pair on a nightly basis and just hope that eventually the feelings of guilt would subside. I'm happy to report that, after a few months, they did.

Chapter 17

Chumbawamba – 'Tubthumping'

'I get knocked down, but I get back up again, you're never gonna keep me down . . .' This has really helped me in some more difficult times and become something of a mantra. I did, however, once see lead singer, Danbert Nobacon, in a charity boxing match against Michaela Strachan. She caught him early with a jab and let's just say 'never meet your heroes'.

Not having a job came as a real shock to the system to me. I realised early on that unemployment is like a very hot bath – you need to ease yourself into it gently but, once you do, you spend a lot of time lying down rubbing your balls. I was still getting up early because of the way my body clock was set. I'm a creature of habit, so I was still conducting my usual routine of vocal exercises and looking for split ends. I think that a sign of professionalism is treating every task with the same rigour and respect, so this was something that I took into my new life. I may not have been broadcasting to millions any more, but that was no reason for my voice and hair to not be glowing. I think that Simon in the corner shop was a bit overwhelmed by my morning trips for the paper at first. He gently taught me that having a conversation with somebody is very different to broadcasting at them and I was a pretty quick learner, even if I do say so myself. Within weeks, he had taught me to go from three hours of high-energy chat, introductions and traffic updates to warm nods and a gentle 'Y'all right?'

A sudden burst of freedom can be quite intimidating. I've heard people talk about coming out of prison and struggling to adapt to a life not constrained by the rules within porridge (prison) which is ironic and sadly leads to them often going back inside stir (prison). I've never been to the slammer (prison) but am pretty sure that if I ever found myself in the big house (prison), I'd do everything I could not to wind up back in the big-bedroom-of-bad-blokes (prison). That said, though, I would nearly end up inside – but more on that later.

I was victim to panic attacks thanks to the big, open expanses of time. They were normally at their worst at the top of the hour when I would suddenly panic that I hadn't led into the news. One day, I even found myself about to get on a train to Glasgow to go for a recording but, thankfully, I realised just in time. It had been presumptuous and probably a waste of time to write recording dates into my diary for the next fifteen years but, if I went back, I doubt I'd do anything differently.

Everybody kept telling me to take a bit of time for myself. 'It's the universe telling you to take a break,' Uri Geller told me. 'When did you last properly rest and give yourself time to unwind?' Toyah Wilcox asked me. 'When did you last take a holiday?' queried my travel agent. It took me a while, but I eventually managed to unwind and really began to embrace it.

Once you get over the panic of never working again, it's quite easy to settle into the life of a house bachelor. I considered being a house husband for a while but cleaning takes ages and there are professional cooks who will deliver food that's nicer than the stuff I make. I began to realise that, used correctly, a lack of structure is a gift. Yes, it can be a disaster like a Neil Buchanan attempt at building a gazebo, but it can also lead to real beauty like a Graham Thorpe scat poem.

With each day a blank canvas, there are untold adventures to be had. No two days are the same and, once you realise that, it becomes quite exhilarating. The diaries I kept were put away in the attic for years but it's been a real thrill to rediscover them. Here are a couple of extracts from days that I've picked at random:

Monday 4th March

Got up at 7.16. Did some stretches and went down for breakfast. Put luxury brand cereal in bowl and added milk. Flicked through full Sky package to watch something for about half an hour. Went and bought some new running gear and walked clockwise around the park at a brisk pace. Stopped in a café for a couple of glasses of Pinot Grigio and some king prawn linguine. Spent the afternoon coming up with new TV vehicle ideas. Defended decision not to do any cleaning in the house and went to bed early in uncomfortable silence.

Tuesday 17th May

Got up at 7.14. Did some stretches and went down for breakfast. Put milk in bowl and added supermarket own-brand cereal. Flicked through Sky basic package to watch something for about twenty-five minutes. Found cleanest running gear without holes and walked anti-clockwise round the park at a brisk pace. Stopped in a café for a cheese panini and some soda water and cordial. Spent the afternoon thinking about my TV vehicle ideas. Defended decision not to do any washing and went to bed early after stilted conversation.

Pretty varied, I think you'll agree. Like two snowflakes or singles by the Lighthouse Family – almost impossible to tell apart on the surface but actually incredibly different in every way to the seasoned observer.

I remember once reading an interview with the writer of *Groundhog Day* and he said he thought the reason the film resonates with so many people is because most of us live a variation of the same day over and over again and the trick is adjusting your approach.

People ask me if I was ever worried about money while I wasn't working, but it honestly never crossed my mind. For me, it was more about how my mind was occupied. I suppose it would be disingenuous to say that I had no interest in the fame side of things. I really don't think it was fame itself per se that was driving me, but I wanted to be flicking my hair in the public eye and flouncing around in its consciousness. I do feel that was more to do with wanting to be doing what I'm good at and seeing fame as a by-product rather than simply chasing the middle pages of a newspaper.

I know that I've lived a wonderful and charmed life and write these words not in an effort to gain sympathy but because my main rule for this book was honesty. I want every word to be true and I want them all to be my own (see disclaimer).

I feel a bit like a broken record (in that I'm repeating myself and enjoyed my greatest success in an earlier decade) but the fame thing has really always been a by-product of my career rather than its main aim. My level of fame has been a consideration but only because it's a way of measuring where my career is at. It's quite an unwelcome measure because it's inescapable. I can give you the St Albans Easter fête as an example. When

Fun House was on the air, I received a first-class letter (doubly so, in that it had been posted first class and was magnificently executed in its tone and presentation). The letter was inviting me to the fête to both open it and be a judge in the 'marquee event' – the marrow-growing contest. I attended as TV's Pat Sharp.

The year that this chapter documents saw me receive an invitation from the same organisers that had no first-class stamp in the top right-hand corner. It didn't even have an envelope and was deeply impersonal. It would actually be more accurate to call it a flier than an invitation. So it was that I went to the St Albans Easter fête, not as TV's Pat Sharp, but as Pat Sharp.

I was again invited to be a judge in 'the marquee event', but this time it was a large tent-building contest that was poorly attended and I think was very much an afterthought. The person in charge of setting up the one-man panel didn't seem to know who I was. Still, I wiped away my tears like a pro and performed my duty. I wasn't sad to be off the marrow-judging panel (far from it – they had a really thankless task that year as there was nothing to choose between the top three) but I was sad to be reminded that I was no longer at the top of my game. I know celebrity brings with it a whole bunch of perks but, if you're an accountant who has slipped from the peak of their powers, you can go to St Albans Easter fête as a way of forgetting that fact, not as a way of being reminded.

Such reminders are everywhere. On the sound advice of my travel agent, I flew first-class to Paris to stay in a suite at the Four Seasons George V. It was quite soon after the end of *Fun House* and it was as I sat in the back of my chauffeured limousine, sipping Moët and finishing off my lobster and truffle croissant that I first came to terms with the fact that I was now unemployed and began to understand exactly what that means for millions of people struggling without work across the globe. I also felt slightly disappointed having not been around to see the Four Seasons George I to IV, but think I was able to get up to speed.

I went to the Eiffel Tower because I'd missed out on the chance when I presented the gala opening of Disneyland Paris in 1992 after a very heated row with the bloke in the Mickey Mouse outfit, which got excessively violent. I also opted for an Eiffel eyeful because I lost confidence in my ability to say 'The Louvre' with a competent pronunciation to my driver. The Eiffel Tower is pretty cool actually and I enjoyed being up there. The views were really nice and I enjoyed thinking that somebody somewhere could well have been taking a picture to be used for postcards or something and that I would be in that photo, which I think is a lovely thing. I think about it whenever I see postcards from Paris but, even using a microscope, I'm still yet to spot myself.

A man nearly tripped me up as I moved around the viewing platform but it appeared to be an accident. His focus was mostly on the girl he was kneeling in front of, rather than me. He produced a ring, she cried and they embraced. With their hands trembling just out of unison, he clumsily slipped the ring on her finger. They laughed and embraced again with tears running down their cheeks. They wiped the tears from each other's eyes instinctively and simultaneously and laughed before embracing again. Looking like he'd forgotten something, the man fumbled in his pocket and produced a camera. He glanced around anxiously and nearly spoke to a few people as they passed by but lost his nerve. He continued to flit his eyes and search until they settled on me. I smiled and he looked thrilled. The happiest moment of his life and I was delighted to witness it and for him to witness me witnessing it. His eyes looked like they would pop with happiness and I gave a quick flick of the hair above my right ear readying myself. 'Would you mind?' he asked, but I was already warming up my cheeks for the big grin that would be the centrepiece of this photo that they would show children and grandchildren and probably strangers in pubs should one of them end up alone. Then he handed me the camera and asked me to take a photo. My cheeks filled with red and my world fell apart.

I really didn't want these things to affect me. I knew that I was a deeply lucky man. There were so many people worse off than me: starving children in Ethiopia, single mothers on council estates, Neil Buchanan; but I was beginning to become depressed. The worst thing was that I was starting to take it out on other people. I caught myself being rude to a shopkeeper. I'd bought a pint of milk – not because I needed it but because Kenny Everett once told me that you should buy it regularly in case anybody ever asks you how much it costs. I'm not entirely sure why, but you don't question Kenny. I bought the milk and the shopkeeper gave me my change. It's actually a little hard to type this and I now can't really believe that the words came out of my mouth. They say that memory is an unreliable thing and I have wondered if I really said what I think I said but that is probably me just trying to let myself off. I hadn't been sleeping and, to give you some context for the stress I was beginning to feel, I had noticed some hairs blocking the plug hole one day after the seventh hair wash. Still, none of this excuses what I said.

'Thank you.'

That was it. Literally all I said was 'Thank you'. Not, 'Thank you, thanks a lot, cheers . . .' Not 'Thank you, very kind, appreciate it, ta . . .' Not, 'Thank you, my good man, ta muchly, cheers, you're a legend . . .' Literally just 'Thank you'. All that is is punctuation. It's a reflex that you say to lay the foundations before expressing your actual gratitude. I only hope that that charming man, who didn't even need to smile to be friendly, is reading this – (a) for the sales; and (b) so he knows that I'm sorry.

I was equally terse in some of the emails with my agent, which I also regret. I was able to joke about the fact that if I was the recipient of any anger from her then she would have to take 10 per cent of it herself and that broke a lot of the tension between us every single time I said it. This book is intended to be warts and all and, in keeping with that spirit, I wanted to include a series of emails from those dark days. There were many but I think this brief exchange is representative and gives you a good idea of where my professional life was at that point: intensive care!

Monday 8.43
Dear Joyce,
*Hope all is well with you and you're having a great Monday. Just
    checking in really . . .*
Your favourite client
Pat

Monday 15.33

Hello Pat,

So great to hear from you! It's an exciting time I think. Onwards
 and upwards.

Best,

Joyce

Monday 15.36

Hello Joyce,

Agreed! Can't wait for the next chapter.

Yours very excitedly,

Pat

Wednesday 11.21

Hi Pat,

Just wondered if you had any ideas?

Best,

Joyce

Wednesday 11.22

Hi Joyce,

Funny you should say that! When would be good to meet? I can put
 a presentation together. Happy hump day!

Hugs and kisses,

Pat

Friday 14.32

Hi Pat,

Could get something in the diary for two weeks?

Best,

Joyce

Friday 14.34

Afternoon Joyce!

TGIF, am I right?! Could do something sooner actually if you have the time.

Your humble and obliging client,

Pat

Wednesday 9.34

Hi Pat,

Two weeks will be fine. Let's do the 14th at ten.

Best,

Joyce

Wednesday 9.35

Hey Joyce,

Perfect! Hope you had a great weekend.

Best,

Pat

So as you can see, I was a bit of a monster. Unfortunately, the idea that we discussed in that meeting on the 14th never went anywhere. I have always been a little bit fascinated by the theatre. I honestly believe that there is something which exists in the souls of all performers. We are all bound by the same essence and fabric of being. Obviously, there are one or two differences, but the soliloquies of Hamlet at the Globe come from the exact same place as announcing that little Lucy and Hank have won a Crayola set and a day at an abseiling centre. Kenneth Branagh and I have often chatted about our slightly differing views on this theory.

I've not read all of Euripides' plays, but I've done most of the tragedies and a fair few of the comedies. I've got wooden carvings of the two masks of drama on the wall of my dining room at home and we often joke that the comedy one is for when I'm cooking and the tragedy is my wife! To be fair to her, she's a good cook. At worst, she tends to over-season but it's a stretch to liken her cuisine to the strangling of an innocent wife or the deaths by suicide of two young lovers. It was after a carbonara that I had over-salted so much that we were in fits of giggles when I looked at those masks and had my idea.

Yin and Yang, black and white, night and day, good and evil, Hale and Pace. Life is made up of opposites and that is where we get meaning from. You need one to know the other. *Fun House* was lively and hilarious and full of colour and joy. The logical step was to introduce the world to its inverted twin.

The producers were extremely negative about *Boring Flat*. We got quite a long way through the planning process because I believed in it and was willing to invest and yet it was still seen as a lukewarm property by some of the executives. Unfortunately, we met resistance at every turn and, eventually, the project was put out of its misery. I still have a notebook full of the ideas and haven't ruled out trying to bring them to life in one way or another, so look out for games where groups of children rummage through drawers of paperwork to try and find their national insurance number or a slow-paced final round where they stand to win some practical but unflattering grey trousers or an unmarked paperweight.

In time, I realised that I might need to broaden my career options. It was not an easy thing to come to terms with, but I had to accept that maybe my next job wouldn't be a presenting one. It might not even be in showbusiness. Luckily, I knew that my skills were transferable and so it proved. I skilfully insinuated earlier that I nearly ended up in a prison, but you can rest assured that it was on the right side of the bars that I almost ended up.

Deciding to work away from the public eye was actually quite liberating. Like a child entering the Fun House, I had no idea where to turn first. I had only two humble goals: to cheer people up; and to be somewhere where my hair would be appreciated. At first, I thought these criteria might be a bit vague but it wasn't long before I realised that they screamed 'prison guard'. Prison can be hard, so having my infectious energy would really make a difference there; plus they have strict regulations on hairstyles, so I knew the inmates would love to live vicariously through my mane. People I told about it were surprised and asked a lot if I was OK. It was nice that they cared but they did seem to have doubts. Thankfully, my focus was as clear as Andrea Corr's skin. Given the level of naysaying I was subjected to, I suspect that one or two of you may doubt my suitability for the role of a prison officer, so please find attached my CV (I'm still down with the lingo) which I subtly tailored for the role:

Patrick Sharpin Curriculum Vitae
DOB: 12 October 1961
Address: 21 Wheatsheaf Place,
Edgware, London, HA8 TRQ

Personal Statement
The man, the hair, the legend. The voice, the eyes, the legend. The waving, the dancing, the legend. The stonewashed jeans, the three-somes with the twins, the legend. A man who needs no introduction but tends to do one anyway because he's so good at them.

Qualifications

Upper Second-Class Honours Degree in 'keepin' on trucking' from the University of Life

Upper Second-Class Honours Degree in Media Studies from Roehampton University

O-Levels in Maths, English, French, PE

First morning of a First-Aid course

Work Experience

Paper Round – put papers in people's letterboxes, taking great care to keep the papers safe and smoothly manage their introduction to a new environment.

BBC Radio 1 DJ – entertained millions and communicated clearly and effectively in all kinds of situations. Was able to put myself in other people's shoes and understand them. Statistically, many of these people would have been prisoners.

BBC Top of the Pops *Presenter – showed self-confidence, integrity and emotional intelligence while introducing some of the hottest acts around. Got used to crowd control and can happily say there was not a single riot, nor shiv-based injury.*

Presenter of Fun House *– worked in an integrated way to keep the communities of contestants safer and allowed the men and women working with them to change their lives. Commissioned and delivered contestant management services in the community and studio to implement orders of the courts and support rehabilitation. I was responsible for supervising and controlling contestants in a decent, legal, safe and sound environment, ensuring that prison procedures were working effectively.*

I was told that everybody lies on CVs, which was why I decided to throw in the twins thing and the uni one. I was certain it would sweeten the deal because inmates would surely behave in exchange for me regaling them with salacious and entirely fictional details honed in nightclubs up and down the country.

I never did hear back about my application but, in the end, it didn't even matter. From out of nowhere, the next stage of my career slipped into gear and I was instantly very excited. I had been worried that I was being washed up after my years in the storm of fame, but I soon realised I was only in the eye of it (like that bit in the film *Twister*). The wind of time kept blowing and I was soon to be caught up in a tornado of relevance. Enough time had passed for nostalgia to kick in – it's a small step from being a nobody to a novelty, and I was about to change my 'bod' to a 'velt'.

Chapter 18

The Buggles – 'Video Killed the Radio Star'

The first video ever on MTV, this always makes me realise how lucky I was to make the difficult transition between mediums. I also like that it doesn't sound dated because when they say, 'I heard you on the wireless back in '62 . . .', people just assume it's about streaming on the Internet.

Some 'journalists' have characterised my time away from TV as my 'wilderness' years but I've never taken offence. If anything, it's a compliment. A wilderness is an uncultivated, uninhabited and inhospitable region, but it's still worth exploring. Certain countries were once considered little more than wildernesses – or is it wilderni? . . . maybe wildernus? – and now they are so advanced that they have things like bowling alleys and KFC delivery. Milton Keynes was once just empty land, but look at it now. Plus I was spending my time wisely – in 2004 alone, I completed Metal Gear Solid and Resident Evil and only occasionally resorted to a guidebook full of cheats (who's got two thumbs covered in blisters and loads of unlocked extras? This guy).

I never really had much time for reality TV prior to getting involved with it. For me, all TV is reality TV. Sure, *Fun House* didn't go out live but the kids were real, the emotions were real, my hair was real. Why should a distinction be drawn between the two? It's the same with all great art – critics like to suggest certain paintings are somehow more significant than others, but is there really all that much difference between the *Beano* and a Monet other than the fact that the former contains better jokes?

When the call came through from my agent about *Celebrity Come Dine with Me*, my initial reaction was excitement, but that's purely because I'd left a series of unanswered voicemails stretching back over a number of months and feared I'd never hear from her again. When she actually told me what the call was concerning, however, I was horrified. I snapped: 'I'm not ready to go on some pathetic "Who remembers . . .?" version of a TV show with a bunch of other washed-up celebs from the '90s! I'm still relevant and I should be on the regular *Come Dine with Me!*'

Joyce is a great agent and she talked me round after mentioning there would be an appearance fee and that I'd be able to use the gag when I say 'I can't stand the heat' then run out of the kitchen in a mock panic.

The contestants on my edition of the show were far from a bunch of washed-up celebs from the '90s so I needn't have worried on that score. I was joined by Michael Barrymore, Jenny Powell and Anthea Redfern, so this would prove closer to the Algonquin Round Table than the average slice of reality TV.

This was 2010 and, obviously, there was some trepidation when it came to visiting Barrymore's home. We'd all heard the stories and it would be a lie to suggest I walked into that house with anything but fear in my heart. I'm extremely sorry to have to report that the rumours were all true and it was exactly as I'd feared – the thermostat was far too high, the chicken was over-seasoned and Michael was generally a pretty poor host for the evening.

When it came for my turn to host, I had a trick up my sleeve. When *Fun House* ended, I made the financially crippling but undoubtedly sensible decision to buy the set and store it in a warehouse in East London. I'd always maintained that you never know just when a ball pond and a series of brightly coloured obstacle courses would come in handy. My beautiful wife had vehemently disagreed but she'd be wolfing down humble pie while Michael, Jenny and Anthea tucked into my infamous Lancashire hotpot.

At least that's what I thought. Unfortunately, the Channel 4 producers didn't like my suggestion that the guests would have to make their way through various decade-old obstacles and gunge in order to sit down for dinner and vetoed the suggestion outright. My wife insisted she'd been right all along, but I still feel I won that argument. If it wasn't for the pig-headedness of a select group of television executives, that investment would have been a shrewd one. If you watch the footage now, you'll just see a group of people having a meal in a boring old dining room and one man, with spectacular hair, holding back tears and dishing out carrots.

The funny thing you learn doing these shows is quite how different the experience is when you're living it as opposed to simply watching it on the box. For instance, that guy who makes the sarcastic comments on *Come Dine with Me* actually sits in the corner of the room off camera commenting on events as they unfold. Everyone just assumes it's done in post-production, but it's not. I cannot tell you how many takes were spoiled by Jenny telling him to 'get fucked' after unflattering remarks about the way she dressed both her salad and body. He said there was way too much mustard in both her vinaigrette and cardigan and she actually swung for him. The problem when you've been off the screen for a while is rolling with the punches and ignoring the steady stream of abuse that comes with the territory.

It was a similar story when I was on *The Weakest Link*. I knew Anne Robinson would employ her stern but sexy headmistress shtick and that she was likely to be more scathing than ever in a room positively brimming with fellow professionals. What I didn't expect was what occurred when I walked past her dressing room half an hour before show time.

'Come on, Anne, come on. You can do this.'

The door was slightly ajar and I decided to take a peek. She was talking to herself and seemingly trying to psych herself up like Robert De Niro in *Taxi Driver*, except instead of wanting to wash the scum off the streets, she was practising saying things like 'Who's the rotten tooth that needs to be pulled?' or 'Who's the one who only gets asked to play five-a-side when people are struggling so much for numbers that the game is in jeopardy and nobody will actually pass them the ball and the other nine all secretly arrange a drink afterwards so they can moan about how they pretty much ruined the game with their missed passes and inability to make even one save on their turn in goal.'

The second one was my idea but she was reluctant to use it for some reason. Seeing that her natural instinct was meekness touched me more than she'll ever know. We are all of us wearing a mask and Anne's just happens to be that of a grump who has mistaken a lemon for an apple and just taken a big old bite. I lost count of the amount of takes we did that day spoiled by Anne starting to say things like 'Who's the snowflake on a beautiful winter's day . . .?' before the director angrily screamed 'Cut!' for the umpteenth time. It's much the same with the bloke in the Ronseal adverts – he actually went to Eton and then RADA. In television, as in life, quite a lot of pretending is involved.

Obviously, once you've done a couple of these shows then the offers start rolling in and people think you'll get involved with any old rubbish. I was determined not to dilute my stock and become known simply as the kind of person who is constantly popping up on reality TV shows. I decided the best bet was for me to whittle it down to a very tight list of all the shows I truly respected and agree only to appear on those. That way, nobody could ever accuse me of spreading myself a bit thin. I'm proud to say I stuck to my guns and, since *Fun House* finished, the only shows I've appeared on are *You Bet!*, *Surprise Surprise*, *Celebrity Squares*, *Banzai*, *The Weakest Link*, *Never Mind the Buzzcocks*, *The Games*, *X-Tra Factor: Battle of the Stars*, *Big Brother's Big Mouth*, *Big Brother's Bit on the Side*, and *I'm a Celebrity . . . Get Me Out of Here!* In this business, it's important to be choosy about what work you take on.

There was one memorable occasion after a recording of *Big Brother's Big Mouth* when Russell Brand was kind enough to invite me back to his pad with some fans after the taping. We entered his beautiful Hampstead abode and I headed to the bathroom to freshen up after a gruelling hour's work saying stuff like, 'Imogen is being really spoilt . . .' and 'Peter really seems like a lovely bloke . . .' The general public has no clue the kind of effect such hard graft has on the follicles. I exited the loo 45 minutes later and made my way to the living room only to be confronted by the curious sight of what appeared to be Russell and his admirers engaging in some kind of game of Naked Twister. Balance has never been my strong suit so, naturally, I made my excuses and left.

Never Mind the Buzzcocks was a strange one for me. I was asked to appear on the Identity Parade round with Mick in which some old fogey is placed in a line-up with a bunch of other codgers and the teams have to try and remember which had been an actual popstar once upon a time. Naturally, my involvement was purely aesthetic and Phill Jupitus (Phill with two Ls, he really is a difficult man) and his team were only supposed to guess which one was Mick. As a gag, because I'm Pat Sharp, they put me in at the end of the row. The audience went absolutely bananas when Jack Dee uttered the immortal words, '. . . Or number five, Pat Sharp?' It was an amazing moment and reminded me that this was where I really belonged. It also made up for half of Jedward assuming I was a cleaner backstage.

Probably my most high-profile gig since the end of *Fun House* was *I'm a Celebrity . . . Get Me Out of Here!* I was incredibly eager to take part, but not for the reasons most people assume. This was 2011, a mere twelve years after the end of the show that had made my name and I still had a sneaking suspicion that we were just on a hiatus. When The Eagles broke up in 1980, singer Don Henley said they would play together again 'when Hell freezes over' so, in 1994, when they actually did, the comeback album was called *Hell Freezes Over*. Time is a great healer, as I knew from the time I drunkenly shaved my head in my youth (an incident so traumatic I couldn't bring myself to write about it in detail in these pages) and I knew I had to be ready for the call at any moment.

I spent a lot of time trying to work out how the show could be improved because there was no point bringing *Fun House* back unless we were mixing it up a bit. Like Darwin and David Duchovny's agent, I think evolution is a great idea. The same thing every week for a decade works really well, but people can get a bit bored of it when you return for that difficult twelfth series. When the call came through from the *I'm a Celebrity . . .* people, I knew it was something I had to do because I had to experience what it was like on the other side of the metaphorical coin. Yes, I'd been collateral damage and had had the occasional gunge hit, but I'd never been a contestant in the truest sense of the word. Added to that is the fact that I was adamant the one thing the show had been missing was venomous snakes and I needed to find out if I was right. I explained over the phone that I was only willing to take part because it'd be vital research and the response I received was, 'Yeah, whatever.' I told the producers to keep my motives quiet and, to be fair to them, they never said a word. There are some nice guys in this business, whatever people might think.

The whole experience was a bit of a blur, just as I imagine it was for PJ and Duncan (probably quite frustrating, too, as everybody kept calling them by the wrong names, which I found horribly awkward and now wish I'd stood up for them and said something). Ironically, this was Series 11 for the show; the very number *Fun House* will be when it returns. Freddie Starr withdrew after a couple of days following an allergic reaction during the 'Greasy Spoon' trial. His delicate tummy shocked me profoundly – this from a man I'd been led to believe favoured a predominantly hamster-based diet. I was eliminated on Day 14 after a bushtucker trial against Fatima Whitbread and left with my head held high and my mouth full of disgusting insects. It was an invaluable experience and I learned a great many things that I'm sure will reveal themselves at some stage.

That bruising encounter with Fatty (my nickname for Fatima that she inexplicably wasn't all that keen on) wasn't my first brush with the Olympics. In 2004, I took part in *The Games*, the Channel 4 show in which a group of celebrities competed in Olympic-style events. They say every experience helps build character in some way, but they're wrong; that was a total waste of time and just a bit rubbish.

One thing I knew is that I couldn't do these shows for the rest of my life. I needed something more rewarding to come along, even if the exploration on *Banzai* of whether I could stay underwater for longer than a genuine German was undoubtedly an important moment in the history of the medium. It was during this period that I realised I had a bright future behind me and started to wonder about the one that stretched out in front of me.

Chapter 19

Suzanne Vega – 'My Name Is Luka'

I met Suzanne once and she was lovely. Richard Ashcroft once told me she had toyed with being called Suzanne Zangief or Suzanne M Bison, but I didn't have the nerve to ask her if it was true, so I guess we'll never know.

It's funny to think about the future. In a way, it doesn't really mean anything. Nobody knows what's going to happen so it feels a bit redundant to be either anxious or excited. It's like speculating about which cards are going to be dealt in a game of gin rummy, but then never bothering to deal the cards. Or to put it another way, I don't have a pension.

I had a decent run on the popular television programme *Never Mind the Buzzcocks*, but it did give me a sense of perspective. Even though I was really enjoying those student gigs, I was always aware in the back of my mind that they would end. That's true of all things, even those summer days that seemed to last for ever as a child . . . and Bruce Forsyth. Each September, I would treat the first gig of freshers' week with trepidation. What if this was the year that they didn't know who I was? I would wait in the wings and dry heave. I'm not sure why all nightclub green rooms smell so strongly of body odour and vomit, but it's something that you never get used to. As my name was announced, my stomach caterpillars would emerge from their cocoons and have a bit of a flap about. Thankfully, they would disperse once I heard a loud cheer of recognition and I would bounce on to the stage waving my way even further into the crowds' hearts.

Eventually, the inevitable happened. I knew immediately that the warm welcome I received was a mindless response to the – admittedly solid – MC work by the resident DJ and not an emotional response to my presence. I wet heaved a little into my mouth and bounced on to the stage with all the vim I could muster. I tried to convince myself that I was imagining it, that they were here for TV's Pat Sharp . . . and I decided to go for it.

'Good evening, Cheltenham! Who's ready to Re-run the . . .' I left the pause and raised my arms to welcome the end of the catchphrase from the capacity crowd. Somebody actually coughed. Silence is a crime in our line of work and I knew then that the student nights dream was over. I gave out the last of my t-shirts, took one last look around the room and took a deep breath so I could get my things from the changing room without having to smell it.

I did move on to the mature student circuit for a short time, but it was never quite the same. The crowds were always smaller and generally weren't drinking. If you're not ten years old and/ or a little bit inebriated, I can see how you might be less inclined to make some noise and be enthralled by the concept of being given points. I would ask the usual questions like 'How are you all doing?' or 'Who's up for a good time?' but instead of cheers or guttural noises, I would receive softly spoken, eloquent responses: 'Not too bad . . . I've got a conference on Thursday and I'm a little worried from the look of the abstracts of the other papers being presented that I'm a bit too focused on Anglo–Asian relationships, but I'm still looking forward to it . . .' or 'I'm teaching at 9.00 over at the Winchester campus so will probably look to make a move before too long.'

Quite often, I would end up having a bit of a chat with the handful of attendees. I didn't give away a single free shot but I did learn quite a lot about the challenges of acquiring Arts and Humanities Research Council funding.

I think I was always meant to go back to radio. In many ways, I never left and I certainly didn't give up my exercises. My voice was still in exquisite condition and my fingers still supple enough to make the faders dance their merry dance to my instruction. At least they would have done if we still had faders. When I took the gig at London's Heart, I was taken aback to see all the computer monitors. It seemed like a betrayal of the classic equipment of the past to me. We have a lot to thank computers for – doing maths for us, spider solitaire and bringing Garry Kasparov down a peg or two, to name just three. You may think losing the classic soundboard from a radio station is a small price to pay for these wonders, but it hit me hard. This rejection of old-school technology was taken to laughable lengths when I saw that they didn't have any chairs.

'Yeah, everyone stands now,' Rosalind, my new producer, told me. So I stood. I stood in front of a soulless monitor and did the Top 10 at 10. The first year we did was 1987 and I thought it was a bit too easy. I begged them not to open with Whitney's 'I Wanna Dance with Somebody' but Rosalind was unmoved.

'I didn't know what year that was,' she said with a shrug.

'You didn't know that chairs are essential furniture,' I wanted to shout but, instead, introduced my listenership to 'Is This Love?' by Whitesnake, using the line, 'They "adder" hit with "Here I Go Again" in 1982 but, in this year, Whitesnake wanted to know "Is This Love?" . . .' Rosalind didn't even titter. It wasn't my best work but it deserved something.

I spent a couple of weeks hating the new systems. I vented some of my frustrations by hitting the touchscreen with more force than was necessary and, when nobody was looking, I'd give the stand a little kick, which ultimately hurt me more than the machine. I did try to adapt to the new systems and questionable playlists and never let my veneer of professionalism slip. Ironically, my heart wasn't in it a lot of the time at London's Heart – a line that I used to great effect in many social situations but had to live with the fact that I could never use it on air. I looked around the studio that didn't feel like a studio. It wasn't the safe cocoon that I was used to. There were no records or CDs surrounding me, no cosy coffee-stained carpet (drinks were not permitted) and everything was glass instead of charming sound-proof cladding. I didn't think there was anything left for them to take. I was wrong. They took the studio. *The studio.*

The rise of Internet radio and digital stations meant that competition was fierce and, when competition is fierce, purse strings get tightened. If it was at all possible to make cuts, then they were made. Lunch was no longer provided; freebies were sold on rather than taken home. I don't know who had the idea to do without a studio, but I hope that they never meet my wife. I suspect they would reach into her chest, grab her beating organ and yank it out, because theirs is clearly the business of ripping the heart out of things that I love.

A lot of people like the idea of working from home. I liked being able to joke about the commute being a nightmare from my bedroom to the bathroom but, in reality, I didn't like the set-up at all. It sounds like a great adventure to be able to work in your dressing gown, but it's strangely unsatisfying. Sure, it's a novelty for a time but it's easy to become a little depressed. The acoustics were best in the bathroom, which I think was to do with the thick shagpile carpet. I joked that it was clearly the most appropriate room to be a radio studio because it was the only one that didn't have a chair in it but, try as I might, I simply couldn't find the correct audience for that observation. Until now.

All I needed was a laptop that I plugged a microphone head-set into and I could record and upload my links. I did it sitting on the toilet (lid down, trousers on) and did get a little bit of that thrill you have when you're on the phone to somebody and they don't realise that you're going to the toilet. I was still working in radio and I was thankful for that. It was so lonely, though. It was funny to think of all the hours I had spent staring into my bathroom mirror as a child. I must have been there for hours, and though most of that time was gazing at my hair, a lot of it was dreaming of broadcasting. Now here I was, still staring at the bathroom mirror, but this time actually broadcasting. All these years later, I'd come full circle. And I was doing it years before social isolation and government-mandated lockdowns made it obligatory for most broadcasters.

They say the darkest hour comes before the dawn and I can confirm that. I was awake at 4am and it was pitch-black. I stubbed my toe on the way to the toilet but, when I got up an hour later, it was light enough for me to see what I was doing and clean up the blood. As I was on my hands and knees, I had an epiphany that would change the way I lived my life – I would start buying carpets with colours based on what I was most likely to spill on them. Lounge is probably red wine, so go for a red carpet. Breakfast room is probably coffee, so I'd go for a brown. The other option would be to have black everywhere. After pricing some black carpets, I had another epiphany. I needed to embrace new technologies. Radio was changing, the industry was changing. It wasn't enough just to ride that wave – I had to be on it as soon as it first started to swell. I needed to see what the future was and get in on the ground floor.

Broadcasting was becoming more remote. The fact that I could do it from my bathroom without very much in the way of equipment made me feel that the future was likely to be on the move. It would be fast and fluid, but how could I capture that? How could having a sense of this be a benefit? I was doing some cursory reading and then it hit me – podcasts. I realised that podcasts were going to be the future and finished reading that article about podcasts and sat down to do some planning.

The more I thought about it, the more obvious it seemed. What is the best thing about radio? The fact that it's live, that you're connected to millions of people. You live your own lives but do so in synchronicity, a fleeting shared experience. So in the future, where it seems that all things are going to be bad, this is the aspect of radio that will be removed. Everything will be pre-recorded. We will have little bitesize disposable chunks that people can listen to whenever they feel like it in isolation and humanity can continue to develop the giant chasms between people that are probably going to lead to the end times. This was obviously a depressing thought to be having but, at the same time, it was pretty exhilarating to feel on the cusp of something new and like my career was about to be back on track. Swings and roundabouts.

Podcasts were still a new thing when I had the idea after reading that article. I could tell that the world would catch up soon, so I needed to get in quick. It's like Stephen Fry – he got to be the first person on Twitter and, as a result, got loads of followers. The hardest part was trying to find a topic for my podcast. I wanted it to be something that had wide appeal. I thought the best thing would be to target every single person. Obviously seven-and-a-half billion listeners was ambitious, but a 30 per cent return felt achievable and would lead to a pretty healthy amount of advertising revenue.

My first podcast was recorded, produced and edited in the bathroom. It was simply titled *Pat Sharp – Life*. In it, I discussed my new carpet idea and the evils of dry shampoo. I was able to keep the carpet chat to a tight five minutes, which I edited down to just over three, but the final recording was still eleven-and-a-half hours. Still, it went online and is probably still there somewhere. For the second episode, I thought that maybe the title was a bit too vague. Sure, we all have life (notice that I didn't say 'a life', Neil Buchanan) but that doesn't seem to be enough of a hook. I needed something less abstract but equally unifying. Like so many great ideas, it came on the toilet, and episode one of *Pat Sharp – Pooing* clocked in at a concise six hours. There was some good stuff about logistics and dietary recommendations, but the pod also covered a range of topics from the optimum width of teeth on a comb and the best way to get out of a floor-level go-kart with dignity, even though it's designed for a child.

I am absolutely certain that my podcasts were up before Stephen Fry's but, once again, he won the battle and his downloads were considerably higher than mine. Rather than being disheartened by this, I took inspiration and vowed to work harder and perfect my craft. I began to think that I had been going about it entirely the wrong way. I saw some of the popular podcasts and realised that they weren't anywhere near as universal as mine. In fact, they were the opposite. People picked incredibly specific topics and it appeared that these were the secret of their success. One podcast was about the television programme *Teen Wolf* and another was about a sex book written by somebody's dad.

I decided to follow suit and the topic was staring me right in the face. The more I read into it, the clearer it was to me that people wanted podcasts about cult subjects. A lot of the popular ones were all about nostalgia. I grinned for hours when I realised what I needed to do. It wasn't as big as some, but I had a name, I had a hook.

Episode 1 of *Pat Sharp's Keeping Up Appearances Series 2, Episode 3* podcast was a success. I was worried that I'd left it too late but, remarkably, I was still the first person to spend four hours dissecting 'The Candlelight Supper'. We all know that Hyacinth Bucket (pronounced bouquet) is obsessed with her candlelight suppers, and it's one of the best recurring motifs in any sitcom. I'm not proud to say that I do allow myself a little smirk sometimes when I think of all the people who think to make this podcast and then see that it's already taken.

In the first episode, I discussed the plot in detail. Episode 2 was spent speculating about whether planning the supper to woo Emmet and land a role in his upcoming light operatic production was Mrs B's best course of action. The third episode was seven hours on what I felt were the menus that Hyacinth considered but rejected. Obviously, there isn't time to talk you through all eighty-seven episodes of *Pat Sharp's Keeping Up Appearances Series 2, Episode 3* podcast. If you're going to go and look them up, I obviously recommend you work through them all, but I do think the highlights are Episode 47, which focuses on Stuart Sherwin's memorable performance as 'Man with Dog', and Episode 62, which unpicks the slapstick training that Josephine Tewson undertook to really nail those scenes where her character Elizabeth spills the coffee because Hyacinth makes her jump.

The podcast didn't kick-start my career. I'd had several emails from Andi Peters about going for lunch but I'd never wanted to. I was trying to look forwards. I didn't want my career to be over and it didn't seem healthy to go and have a conversation that would have mainly involved reminiscing and celebrating past glories rather than trying to create new ones. It's the same reason I never meet up with my exes. Eventually, though, I caved and went to Pizza Express with him and Floella Benjamin. The mood was a little bit tense because we realised that we had all forgotten to bring vouchers and had to eat Sloppy Giuseppes that were no better than fine at full price. We got over that, though, and had a lovely time – far better than I could have even hoped. We still go for dinner and we don't talk about the old days, but we know they're there and that's enough.

I do look back sometimes. It's often when I'm spending a Sunday afternoon in the garden or reversing the car and I think it's a good thing to do on occasion. The past is a bit like

Stevenage – you don't want to live in it but you shouldn't ignore it completely. They say that sometimes you have to take a step backwards to take two steps forwards (presumably, these are the people you find walking through shopping centres on the weekends) and I truly believe that.

One afternoon, I was clearing out some old boxes and I found a bunch of letters. They were largely fan mail, although nestled among them was my prized letter from Sir Terry. Folded inside that letter was another letter. I reread Sir Terry's and found myself getting a little choked up, then unfolded the letter secreted within it that I'd completely forgotten about . . . and I nearly asphyxiated. This is what it said:

> *Dear Patman,*
>
> *Thank you so much for replying to my letter and for all those sachets of shampoo. Your kind words about my tape meant an awful lot and I've gone to my local hospital radio station to be a volunteer. I play Pat and Mick every show! Thank you for the cheque, although I don't think mobile discos exist any more and it's probably nowhere near enough money . . . but I do appreciate it.*
>
> *Your friend and hopefully future colleague,*
>
> *Greg James, 12/11/2000*

I can tell you that even hosting *Fun House* doesn't compare to momentarily feeling like Terry Wogan.

Epilogue

B★Witched – 'C'est la Vie'

For me, this is peak '90s – catchy, quality pop from a girlband wearing denim. Just makes you want to jump up and down. Whenever I hear this, it just is the '90s again. Also, without it, I never would have learned that 'bewitched' is a swear word in Ireland.

Endings are never easy, especially when the television staple 'see you next time . . .' no longer applies. A life is a very difficult thing to get a sense of. It is 25 October 2019, my fifty-eighth birthday; I fear a midlife crisis might be imminent but my wife says I'm far too old for that. Since I plan to live until at least 116, she's wrong. I bite my tongue and think of happier times.

To celebrate the occasion, she has invited a few friends, family members and hairdressers around to celebrate, even though I'm not really in the mood. I've been thinking about my recent gigs and the transition I seem to have made from 'cheese' nights to 'shite' ones. There are only so many times one can see a poster dominated by cartoon poos and the words 'Absolute Shite – simply the worst – guaranteed (featuring Pat Sharp)' before it starts to feel, well, shite. Especially when the pre-programmed playlist features the music of Pat and Mick despite earlier assurances to the contrary.

This train of thought is interrupted by the sound of extremely loud music. For some reason, the missus extended the invite to

Neil Buchanan (possibly because we were born in the same month and he needs to latch on to someone else's birthday if anyone is going to show up) and he is playing with his heavy metal band, Marseille. My love of music is well documented, both in these pages and a variety of Sky music channel top 50 lists, but I simply can't stand metal. I think it stems from an unfortunate childhood experience with cobalt. My head pounds and I fight back the tears as they play non-stop for the next three hours. This is a low.

The worst part of all this is that I had a very specific idea about how I wanted my birthday to go down this year. I dropped subtle hints to my wife about something with a *Fun House* theme . . . like asking her for a party with a *Fun House* theme. Instead, I've ended up with a blinding headache, flash-backs to embarrassing chemistry lessons and an intervention.

That's right, an intervention. My nearest and dearest gather round me when the cake is brought out and tell me, in no uncertain turns, that it's over. *Fun House* isn't coming back. I will not be given the chance to revive the show in any form. It's time to move on. I inhale deeply and extinguish all 58 candles with one almighty blow. Despite everything, I still make a wish my loved ones almost certainly wouldn't approve of.

As I slump in my favourite chair and contemplate the futility of existence, Neil comes over with a card.

'It's from all of us.'

I open it slowly and without joy, not dissimilar to Neil's method of presenting. What I see shocks me more than anything they ever showed on *How 2*.

It's a flyer. For a gig. A gig I agreed to DJ at months ago:

'80s Nostalgia Party
All your favourite hits from all your favourite artists
Unlimited drinks from 1pm until 6pm
Including Rick Astley, Bananarama, Toyah,
Jason Donovan, Duran Duran and more
Plus guest DJ Pat Sharp playing massive '80s tunes!

It isn't that flyer that shocks me. It is the flyer that is paper-clipped to the back of it. It is tattered, the colour faded and it uses a font that probably hasn't been available on Microsoft Word for at least 25 years. It is for an event in 1988 and the bill is almost identical. A wall-to-wall line-up of cherished old friends, some of whom I met for the first time that weekend, but all of whom are close to my heart. All of whom I'll get to go and throw a huge party with in the present day.

I don't want it to sound crass, but I do think about how much I got paid for that first gig and what I'm being paid for this one. This one is more. A lot more. A lot more money to go and hang out with old, dear friends to create new memories while reliving the old ones. Past and present, fact and fiction, it all mingles together in my mind and I think I might have an idea for a book . . .

Every new beginning comes from some other beginning's end. I put the pieces of paper down on the coffee table in front of me and wipe away a tear. Neil is laughing. My wife is laughing. Suddenly we're all laughing. This is a fun house.

They say you can never go back.

Fuck 'em.

Let's re-run the fun.

Acknowledgements

Thanks to Ed Wilson at Johnson & Alcock, the only man on earth whose twin passions are P.G. Wodehouse and Metallica. Your wisdom, belief and guidance have been invaluable. We also owe a debt of thanks to Andreas Campomar, Jon Davies, Claire Chesser, Jo Wickham and the team at Little, Brown. First among equals is Pat Sharp, a genuine broadcasting legend – thank you for letting us do this.

Luke Catterson
I'd like to thank my mum, Huw and my grandparents for everything but notably letting me watch *Fun House,* and Darren for making this happen and so much fun. There are many more people whose support, encouragement and patience have made the achievement of this book possible, and it's a fool's errand to try and list them all, but they are loved very much.

Darren Richman
Special thanks to two teachers named David: David Brown, a hero who told me writing was a feasible career when I most needed to hear it and David Hilton, a religious man who said nearly a quarter of a century ago that one day I'd write one of these things – you always had faith.

Thanks to my collaborators of yesteryear: David Rudnick and Matt Greene, both inspirational figures. Matt, your guidance and support over the years have been essential, thank you for that and the proof that not everyone to whom I owe a debt of gratitude is called David.

Thanks to my family and friends for all the encouragement over the years, not least my brother and sister for mockingly referring to me as 'Shakespeare' since my teens in a way that belied their unstinting support.

Thank you to Luke for responding to this idea with the words 'Let's do it' and ensuring this was the most enjoyable project I've ever been involved with. A whole lot of fun, indeed.

Thanks to my mum and dad for everything but especially instilling in me a love of comedy and the written word.

Finally, thanks to my wife and children. Kate, your love and support mean more than I can put into words and hopefully this makes up for my wedding speech consisting almost exclusively of jokes.

Pat Sharp

Firstly, I'd like to thank my hairdresser, wife, shampooist and children. There are a number of things people have given me that have made this book possible: Patience – a big thanks to Take That for the banger that I've listened to on repeat; Time – having a good magazine is a great way to recharge the batteries and Sonia, I'll have your November issue back to you soon; Help – a big thanks to The Beatles for that banger that I've listened to on repeat; love – my dear old mum said you should never date a tennis player because to them love means nothing but my friends and family are not tennis players (apart from

Jeremy Bates) or if they are, they have given me their 15s, 30s, 40s, deuces, tie-breaks and sets.

I've also been lucky enough to get some invaluable advice along the way and will never make a carbonara again without putting a little nutmeg in, nor will I ever forget to fold over the end of the Sellotape – many thanks to Messrs Blobby and Motivator for those.

I'd also like to thank the Harvard University Faculty of Arts and Sciences and Department of Anthology for the access to their wonderful libraries while researching this book. The air fares got out of control but they provided an invaluable resource for more than one sentence.

I'd like to thank my ghostwriters. I have to say being ghosted in this way was a far happier experience than when Michaela Strachan did it to me after that one date.

And, of course, thank you to everyone who made the house so fun, not least Martina and Melanie (or is it Melanie and Martina?).

Index